THE LANGUAGE OF LOGIC

ORIGINAL TITLE:

"EXACTE LOGICA"

De Erven F. Bohn N.V., Haarlem, 1961

THE LANGUAGE
of
LOGIC

by

HANS FREUDENTHAL

Professor of Pure and Applied Mathematics,
Utrecht University, Utrecht, The Netherlands

ELSEVIER PUBLISHING COMPANY
AMSTERDAM/LONDON/NEW YORK 1966

ELSEVIER PUBLISHING COMPANY
335 JAN VAN GALENSTRAAT P.O. BOX 211, AMSTERDAM

AMERICAN ELSEVIER PUBLISHING COMPANY INC.
52 VANDERBILT AVENUE, NEW YORK, N.Y. 10017

ELSEVIER PUBLISHING COMPANY LIMITED
RIPPLESIDE COMMERCIAL ESTATE, BARKING, ESSEX

LIBRARY OF CONGRESS CATALOG CARD NUMBER 65-13895

WITH 6 ILLUSTRATIONS

PRINTED IN THE NETHERLANDS

CONTENTS

1 | SETS AND MAPPINGS

1.1 | *Examples of Sets*

The set of all people (now alive). — The set of all hydrogen atoms. — The set of all positive integers (i.e., 1, 2, 3, ...). — The set of all integers (i.e., ..., − 3, − 2, − 1, 0, 1, 2, 3, ...). — The set of all rational numbers (i.e., in addition to

$$\overset{\displaystyle \sqrt{2}}{\underset{\overset{\bullet}{-1}\quad \overset{\bullet}{0}\quad \overset{\bullet}{1}\quad \overset{\bullet}{2}\quad \overset{\bullet}{3}}{\rule{7cm}{0.4pt}}}$$

the integers, also the fractions of integers, e.g., $\frac{7}{4}$, $-\frac{26}{8}$, etc.). — The set of all real numbers (i.e., also such numbers as $\sqrt{2}$, log 7, π, infinite decimal fractions); this set may also be conceived as the so-called number scale, i.e., a horizontal straight line on which the positive numbers are set out as lengths to the right, and the negative numbers to the left, from a point 0. — The set of all complex numbers (these are numbers of the form $a + bi$ with real a and b and a symbol i representing the non-real square root of -1). — The set of all points X which have the same distance from two fixed points A and B (in plane geometry we speak of "locus" instead of "set"). — The set of all real x which satisfy the condition $-3 \leq x \leq 5$. — The set of all real x which satisfy the equation $x^2 + 1 = 0$; this set contains no number: it is "empty". — The set of the pairs of numbers (x, y) which satisfy $3x + 2y = 6$. — Etc.
We shall not define what a set is, but confine ourselves to examples.

1.2 | *The fundamental relation in set theory is that of "membership"*

3 is a member of the set of natural numbers (also of the set of integers, rational numbers, etc.); $-\frac{26}{8}$ is a member of the set of rational numbers but not of the set of integers, nor of the set of real numbers x which satisfy $-3 \leq x \leq 5$. There is nothing which is a member of the empty set. A set is completely defined if we can tell of every object whether or not it is a member thereof.

"a is a member of A" will henceforth be written: $a \in A$.

"a is not a member of A" is written: $a \notin A$.

"$\in$" is called the *adhesion sign*.

Let A be the set of integers, B the set of real numbers, C the set of English playwrights. Then: $3 \in A$, $3 \in B$, $3 \notin C$; $\sqrt{2} \notin A$, $\sqrt{2} \in B$, $\sqrt{2} \notin C$; Shakespeare $\notin A$, $\notin B$, $\in C$.

The empty set is the set X for which there exists no a with the property $a \in X$ — or in other words: $a \notin X$ for every a.

The empty set is designated by $\bigcirc$.

When are two sets A and B equal? If every a, which is a member of A, is also a member of B, and *vice versa*. In other words: if for every a with $a \in A$ the statement $a \in B$ is also valid, and if for every a with $a \in B$ the statement $a \in A$ is also valid.

This being so, we write $A = B$.

If A and B are not equal, we write $A \neq B$.

1.3 | To be part of / To be contained in

Another important relation is that of "*being included in*" or "*being contained in*" or "*being a subset of*". The set of all British playwrights is contained in (or is included in, or is a subset of) the set of all playwrights. The set of all integers is contained in the set of all real numbers.

"A is contained in B" is written as: $A \subset B$ or $B \supset A$ (or: "A is included in B", or "B contains A"). The sign "$\subset$" is called the *inclusion sign*.

"A is not contained in B" is written as: $A \not\subset B$ or $B \not\supset A$.

Precise definition of "$\subset$": $A \subset B$ means that each a which is a member of A is also a member of B. In other words: for each a with $a \in A$ we also have $a \in B$. If $A \subset B$, but not $A = B$, then we say that A is a *proper subset* of B. According to our definition B itself is also a (improper) subset of B. We have $B \subset B$.

Furthermore: If $A \subset B \subset A$, then $A = B$.

$\qquad\qquad$ If $A \subset B$ and $B \subset C$, then $A \subset C$.

1.4 | Consider the set A with three members Argentina, Brazil, Chile, designated by a, b, c.

So $x \in A$ is true if and only if $x = a$ or $x = b$ or $x = c$. We also write $A = (a, b, c)$. We shall seek all the subsets of A. There are eight of them ($= 2^3$), namely:

$\bigcirc$ (the empty set);

(a) (the set with a as the only member), and similarly (b) and (c);

(a, b) (the set with a and b as the only members), and similarly (a, c) and (b, c);

$(a, b, c) = A$ itself.

Now consider the set B with four members, a, b, c, d.

This has twice as many subsets as A has, because the new member d may or may not be added to each subset of A. By this process we obtain all the subsets of B: from each subset of A we get two subsets of B. Thus B has 2^4 subsets.

Generalizing we find:

A set with n members has 2^n subsets.

This also holds for $n = 0$: the empty set has $2^0 = 1$ subset, namely, the empty set itself (although the empty set has no member).

1.5 | The set of all English families is not the same as the set of all English people. Let A denote the first and B the second set. The members of B are the individual English men and women. No person as such is a member of A, the members of A being families. The one-person families are no exception. The "family" comprising the single Miss Jones as its only member is not the same thing as the individual person Miss Jones. The family of this Miss Jones is a set with exactly one member. On the other hand Miss Jones herself, is not a set. The set B of all English people has about four times as many members as the set A of all English families. Each member of A is a subset of B; in other words: if $c \in A$, then $c \subset B$. However: not every subset of B is also a member of A, but only these subsets of B which are families.

Let C be a federation of three clubs a, b, c. Let a have the members α, β, γ, δ, ε, b the members α, γ, μ, ν, and c the members δ, ϱ, σ, τ. Hence

$$C = (a, b, c)$$
$$a = (\alpha, \beta, \gamma, \delta, \varepsilon), \quad b = (\alpha, \gamma, \mu, \nu), \quad c = (\delta, \varrho, \sigma, \tau).$$

Then $\alpha \in a$, $\beta \in a$, $\gamma \in a$ etc., $\alpha \in b$, $\gamma \in b$ etc., $\delta \in c$, $\varrho \in c$ etc. Also $a \in C$, $b \in C$, $c \in C$. But $\alpha \notin C$, $\beta \notin C$, $\gamma \notin C$, $\mu \notin C$, $\varrho \notin C$ etc.

1.6 | The foregoing can be summarized in the following warnings:

Do not confuse a with the set (a) of which a is the only member; (a) has exactly one member, namely, a, while a need not be a set or if it is a set may have no members or one member or more members.

If $\alpha \in a$ and $a \in A$, then it is not necessary at all, that $\alpha \in A$. (It may happen, however — for instance, if A is a federation which includes individual persons as well as clubs among its members, a being one of those clubs and α being a member of a as well as an individual member of the federation A).

Do not confuse "$\in$" and "$\subset$". In the example given in 1.4 we have

$$a \in A, \quad b \in A, \quad c \in A,$$

but *not* $a \subset A$, $b \subset A$, $c \subset A$. Furthermore

$$(a) \subset A, \quad (b) \subset A, \quad (c) \subset A,$$

but *not* $(a) \in A$, $(b) \in A$, $(c) \in A$, etc. Also

$$(a) \subset (a, b),$$

but *not* $(a) \in (a, b)$.

1.7 | Operations on Sets

Certain operations can be applied to sets. Given two sets A and B; from these we can form
  1) their union $A \cup B$,
  2) their intersection $A \cap B$,
  3) the difference $A \setminus B$.
$A \cup B$ means: the two sets thrown together.
$A \cap B$ means: what the two sets have in common.
$A \setminus B$ means: removed from A what belongs to B.
More precisely:

$c \in A \cup B$ means $c \in A$ or*) $c \in B$.
$c \in A \cap B$ means $c \in A$ and $c \in B$.
$c \in A \setminus B$ means $c \in A$ and $c \notin B$.

Examples:
A = set of all male human beings, B = set of all adults, $A \cup B$ = set of all people except girls, $A \cap B$ = set of all male adults, $A \setminus B$ = set of all boys, $B \setminus A$ = set of all (adult) women.
If $A \cap B = \bigcirc$, then A and B are said to be *mutually exclusive* or *disjoint*.
So as not to confuse "$\cup$" and "$\cap$", note that the form of "$\cup$" reminds of the U of "Union".

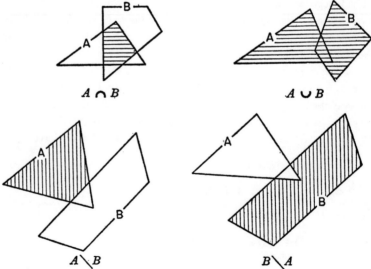

Fig. 1

*) I.e., c may also be a member of both.

1.8 | Laws for " ∪" and "∩ "

The operations with "∪" and "∩" are subject to certain *laws*:

$$A \cup B = B \cup A \qquad \text{(commutativity of "}\cup\text{")}$$
$$(A \cup B) \cup C = A \cup (B \cup C) \qquad \text{(associativity of "}\cup\text{")}$$
$$A \cap B = B \cap A \qquad \text{(commutativity of "}\cap\text{")}$$
$$(A \cap B) \cap C = A \cap (B \cap C) \qquad \text{(associativity of "}\cap\text{")}$$
$$(A \cup B) \cap C = (A \cap C) \cup (B \cap C)$$
$$(A \cap B) \cup C = (A \cup C) \cap (B \cup C) \qquad \text{(distributivities)}$$

The associative laws state that in expressions such as $A \cup B \cup C$ and $A \cap B \cap C$ it does not matter where the parentheses are placed. We shall therefore simply omit them. On the other hand, in expressions such as

$$(A \cup B) \cap C \quad \text{or} \quad A \cup (B \cap C)$$

it does matter where the parentheses are placed. Example: A = set of all men, B = set of all women, C = set of all people over fifty years of age. $A \cup B$ = set of all people, $(A \cup B) \cap C$ = set of all people over fifty years of age, $B \cap C$ = set of all women over fifty years of age, $A \cup (B \cap C)$ = set of all people except women up to fifty years of age.

The above laws are rather like certain arithmetical laws — *viz.*, addition (instead of "∪") and multiplication (instead of "∩"). Only the last law has no arithmetical counterpart.

The first four laws are easy to prove. Here we shall confine ourselves to the proof of the validity of the sixth law (the proof of the fifth law being similar). We must therefore prove that the sets

$$D = (A \cap B) \cup C$$

and

$$E = (A \cup C) \cap (B \cup C)$$

are the same, i.e., that
1) if $x \in D$, then $x \in E$,
2) if $x \in E$, then $x \in D$.
Re 1: Let $x \in (A \cap B) \cup C$.
    Then
    either (α): $x \in A \cap B$
    or (β): $x \in C$.
    In case (α) it holds true that

$$x \in A, \text{ hence also } x \in A \cup C$$

and
$$x \in B, \text{ hence also } x \in B \cup C.$$

From $x \in A \cup C$ and $x \in B \cup C$ follows $x \in (A \cup C) \cap (B \cup C)$.
Hence $x \in E$.
In case (β) $x \in C$, hence $x \in A \cup C$ and $x \in B \cup C$, hence $x \in (A \cup C) \cap (B \cup C)$, hence $x \in E$.

Re 2: Let $\qquad\qquad x \in (A \cup C) \cap (B \cup C)$.

Then		$x \in A \cup C,$
hence	(γ):	$x \in A$ or $x \in C.$
Further		$x \in B \cup C,$
hence	(δ):	$x \in B$ or $x \in C.$
Is $x \in C$, then		$x \in (A \cap B) \cup C$, hence $x \in D.$
Is $x \notin C$, then		
because of (γ)		$x \in A$
and because of (δ)		$x \in B,$
hence		$x \in A \cap B,$
hence		$x \in (A \cap B) \cup C,$
hence		$x \in D.$

Other laws:

$$A \cup O = A, \quad A \cap O = O.$$
$$A \subset A \cup B, \quad A \supset A \cap B.$$

If $A \subset B$, then $A \cup C \subset B \cup C$ and $A \cap C \subset B \cap C$.
If $A \subset C$ and $B \subset C$, then $A \cup B \subset C$.
If $A \subset B$ and $A \subset C$, then $A \subset B \cap C$.

1.9 | Reciprocity Laws

In this section we shall only consider sets which are contained in a particular fixed set T ("total").
Let A be such a set. Then

$$A^* = T \backslash A$$

is called the *complement* of A (with respect to T).
Hence $a \in A^*$ if, and only if, $a \notin A$.

$$O^* = T, \quad T^* = O.$$

It can readily be proved that

$$(A^*)^* = A$$

(i.e., the complement of the complement of A is A itself).

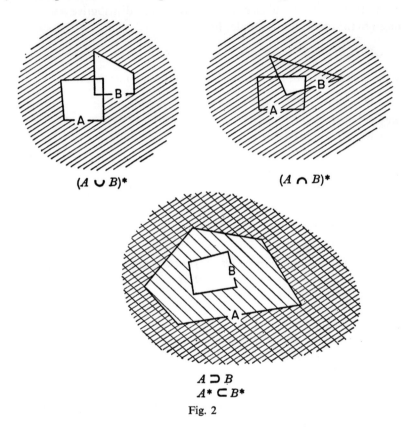

$(A \cup B)^*$ $(A \cap B)^*$

$A \supset B$
$A^* \subset B^*$
Fig. 2

If $A \subset B$, then $A^* \supset B^*$ (1st reciprocity law).

For if $c \in B^*$, then $c \notin B$, therefore $c \notin A$, and therefore $c \in A^*$.

$$(A \cup B)^* = A^* \cap B^* \qquad \text{(2nd reciprocity law)}.$$

Indeed $c \in (A \cup B)^*$, if, and only if, $c \notin A \cup B$. But c is not a member of the union of A and B if, and only if, c is neither in A nor in B, i.e., if $c \in A^*$ and also $c \in B^*$.
Similarly

$$(A \cap B)^* = A^* \cup B^* \qquad \text{(3rd reciprocity law)}.$$

The three laws of reciprocity can also be formulated as follows:

On passing to the complement ("applying the asterisk"), the symbols "$\subset$" and "$\supset$" and also the symbols "$\cup$" and "$\cap$" are interchanged.

By making use of this property we can reduce the commutative law for "$\cup$" to that for "$\cap$", and *vice versa*. Similarly the associative law for "$\cup$" can be reduced to that for "$\cap$", and *vice versa*. Finally, each distributive law can thus be reduced to the other. For example: In

$$(A^* \cup B^*) \cap C^* = (A^* \cap C^*) \cup (B^* \cap C^*)$$

take the complement of the left-hand and right-hand members:

$$(A^* \cup B^*)^* \cup C^{**} = (A^* \cap C^*)^* \cap (B^* \cap C^*)^*,$$
$$\text{hence } (A^{**} \cap B^{**}) \cup C^{**} = (A^{**} \cup C^{**}) \cap (B^{**} \cup C^{**}),$$
$$(A \cap B) \cup C = (A \cup C) \cap (B \cup C).$$

1.10 | Problems

1) Prove for any four sets A, B, C, D:

    a) $A = (A \setminus B) \cup (A \cap B)$,

    b) $A \cup B \cup C = (A \setminus B) \cup (B \setminus C) \cup (C \setminus A) \cup (A \cap B \cap C)$,

    c) $A \cup B \cup C \cup D = (A \setminus B) \cup (B \setminus C) \cup (C \setminus D) \cup (D \setminus A) \cup (A \cap B \cap C \cap D)$.

Prove that:

    a') the sets $A \setminus B$ and $A \cap B$ from a) are disjoint;

    b') every pair of the sets $A \setminus B, B \setminus C, C \setminus A$ and $A \cap B \cap C$ from b) is disjoint;

    c') by means of a counter-example show that not every pair of the sets $A \setminus B, B \setminus C, C \setminus D, D \setminus A, A \cap B \cap C \cap D$ from c) need be disjoint.

2) Prove for any three subsets A, B and C of T:

    a) $A \cup B = A \cup (B \setminus (A \cap B))$.

    b) $A \setminus B = A \cap B^*$.

    c) $A^* \cup (B \cup C)^* = (A \cap B)^* \cap (A \cap C)^*$.

    d) If $A \subset C$, then $A \cup (B \cap C) = (A \cup B) \cap C$ (DEDEKIND's law).

    e) $(A \setminus B) \setminus C = (A \setminus C) \setminus (B \setminus C)$.

    f) $(B \setminus C) \setminus (B \setminus A) \subset A \setminus C \subset (A \setminus B) \cup (B \setminus C)$.

3) Prove for any natural number n and for any n sets $A_1, A_2, \ldots, A_{n-1}, A_n$:

$$A_1 \cup A_2 \cup \ldots \cup A_{n-1} \cup A_n = (A_1 \setminus A_2) \cup (A_2 \setminus A_3) \cup (A_3 \setminus A_4) \cup \ldots$$
$$\ldots \cup (A_{n-1} \setminus A_n) \cup (A_n \setminus A_1) \cup (A_1 \cap A_2 \cap \ldots \cap A_n).$$

1.11 | Mappings

By the *mapping f* of a set A *into* a set B is understood a law whereby to each member x of A is assigned one member y of B. This relation between $X \in A$ and $y \in B$ is designated by

$$y = f(x).$$

Hence x is here a variable member running over the whole of A; in each case y is the "image" of x; f is the sign denoting that particular mapping. It should be noted that, in the present context, "mapping" refers to the process of mapping; what is formed as a result of mapping an *original* x is called the *image* thereof.

(Sometimes mappings are considered, in which more than one y may be assigned to one x. These will not be dealt with in this book, however.)

The concept of "mapping" is a generalisation of the concept of function. For example, let a function f be defined by

(1) $f(x) = 3x^2 - 6x - 9.$

Here A and B are both the set of real numbers. The mapping (function) f assigns to each real number x the image

$$y = 3x^2 - 6x - 9,$$

e.g., to:

the number $x = -1, \quad 0, \quad \tfrac{1}{3}, 3, \dots$
the number $y = \quad 0, \; -9, \; -\tfrac{32}{3}, 0, \dots$

In the case of

(2) $g(x) = \dfrac{1}{x-2}$ (for $x \neq 2$)

a function g is defined, which maps

     A, set of real numbers $\neq 2$, into
     B, set of real numbers.

Other examples:

3) A = set of all bicycles, B = set of all people, f assigns to each bicycle its owner.

4) A = set of all people (alive or deceased), B ditto, f assigns to each person his or her mother.

5) A = set of all people, B = set of all human heads, f assigns to each person his or her head.

1.12 | A mapping f of A into B is called a mapping of A *onto* B if each member of B occurs as an image.

A mapping f of A into B is called *one–one* (or, more briefly: 1–1) if f assigns *different* images in B to *different* members of A.

Hence: f is "onto" if each member of B has *at least* one original in A. f is "1–1" if each member of B has *at most* one original in A.

For the five examples in 1.11 we have:

(1) neither "onto" nor "1–1". For $3x^2 - 6x - 9 = 3(x^2 - 2x - 3) = 3(x - 1)^2 - 12$ is always ≥ -12, since $(x - 1)^2$ is always ≥ 0; -12 is the minimum (which is attained for $x = 1$); $f(x)$ cannot assume lower values; hence not every member of B occurs as an image. f is not a mapping of A onto B. If we had taken for B the set of all real numbers ≥ -12, then f would indeed have been a mapping "onto". f is not "1–1" either, because for example 0 has two originals, -1 and 3.

(2) "1–1", but not "onto". For $\dfrac{1}{x-2}$ will certainly never assume the value 0. However, if $a \neq 0$, then there is precisely one $x \neq 2$ of which a is the image, namely, the x which satisfies $\dfrac{1}{x-2} = a$, or $x = 2 + \dfrac{1}{a}$.

(3) neither "onto" nor "1–1". Because there are people who have no bicycle and there are others who own more than one bicycle.

(4) neither "onto" nor "1–1".

(5) "onto" and "1–1".

1.13 | Given three sets A, B, C, a mapping f of A into B, and a mapping g of B into C. For an $x \in A$ we can look for its f-image $y \in B$, and for the latter we can in turn look for the g-image $z \in C$,

$$z = g(y) = g(f(x)).$$

We thus obtain a mapping h of A into C.

$$h(x) = g(f(x)).$$

This h is known as the composite or *product* of the given mappings and is designated by gf,

$$gf(x) = g(f(x)).$$

Example: A, B, C = set of all people (alive or deceased). f assigns to each person his or her mother. g assigns to each person his or her father. What is gf? What is fg? Are they the same?

A, B, C = set of real numbers. f is defined by $f(x) = x - 2$, g is defined by $g(x) = 3x$. $g(f(x)) = 3f(x) = 3(x - 2) = 3x - 6; f(g(x)) = f(3x) = 3x - 2$.

Caution: It is not possible to combine arbitrary mappings. If we take for f the mapping from 1.11.3 and for g the mapping from 1.11.4, then $gf(x)$ means: the mother of the owner of bicycle x. On the other hand $fg(x)$ (the owner of the mother of the bicycle x) is meaningless. In order to be able to combine mappings f and g into a mapping gf we must require that f maps into the set on which g is defined.

1.14 | Of especial importance is the concept of 1–1-onto-mapping. If f is a 1–1 mapping of A onto B, then for each $y \in B$ there exists exactly one $x \in A$ with $y = f(x)$. By assigning to each $y \in B$ that $x \in A$ for which $y = f(x)$, we obtain a 1–1 mapping g of B onto A, the *inverse* of the given f.
The inverse g of a 1–1 mapping f of A onto B is therefore defined by

$$x = g(y) \text{ if, and only if, } y = f(x).$$

In other words, $gf(x) = x$ for all $x \in A$,

and $fg(y) = y$ for all $y \in B$.

A special 1–1 mapping of a set A onto itself is the identity mapping φ, defined by

$$\varphi(x) = x \text{ for all } x \in A.$$

If g is the inverse of f, then gf and fg are equal to the identity mapping φ.

Examples: A, B = set of real numbers, f defined by $f(x) = 3x + 5$. Then the inverse g of f will be obtained by putting $f(g(x)) = x$, hence $3g(x) + 5 = x$, $g(x) = \frac{1}{3}(x - 5)$.
Let f be the mapping from 1.11.5. The inverse assigns to each human head the person belonging to it.

1.15 | *Cardinal Numbers*

When do we say of two sets A and B that they have equal numbers of members or that one has more or fewer members than the other? How do we ascertain whether there are as many people as chairs in a room? We ask the people to sit on the chairs. If chairs are left vacant, then there are more chairs than people; if all the chairs are occupied and people are left standing, then there are more people than chairs; if everyone is seated and there are no vacant chairs, then the numbers of people and chairs are equal. Sitting down corresponds to effecting (or endeavouring to effect) a 1–1 mapping of the set of people onto the set of chairs.

Definition of cardinal equivalence: Two sets A and B are called *cardinally equivalent* if there exists a 1–1 mapping of A onto B.

(In the statement "*A* and *B* are cardinally equivalent" *A* and *B* play a symmetrical part, whereas in the definition we required the existence of a 1–1 mapping of A onto B. But we know that then there will also exist such a mapping of B onto A, namely, the inverse.)

1.16 | The set of natural numbers

   1, 2, 3, ...

is cardinally equivalent to the set of even numbers

   2, 4, 6, ...

because $f(x) = 2x$ yields the desired f.

Similarly, the set of natural numbers is cardinally equivalent to that of the 1000-folds; also with the set of the numbers > 3000 — we define f by

   $$f(x) = x + 3000.$$

The set N of natural numbers is infinite. Every set A which is cardinally equivalent to N is called *countably* infinite, i.e., we can *count* the members of such an A by means of the natural numbers: we can place them in a row.

The finite and the countably infinite sets together are also called *countable* sets.

The set A of all integers is countably infinite; we can arrange the members of A in a row,

   N: 1, 2,   3, 4,   5, 6,   7, ...
   A: 0, 1, -1, 2, -2, 3, -3, ...

The set A of all rational numbers is countably infinite:

   N: 1, 2,   3, 4,   5, 6,   7, 8,   9, 10,   11, 12,   13, 14,   15,
   A: 0, 1, -1, 2, -2, $\frac{1}{2}$, $-\frac{1}{2}$, 3, -3, $\frac{1}{3}$, $-\frac{1}{3}$, $\frac{2}{3}$, $-\frac{2}{3}$, $\frac{3}{2}$, $-\frac{3}{2}$,

   N: 16, 17, 18, 19, 20, 21, 22, 23, ...
   A: 4, -4, $\frac{1}{4}$, $-\frac{1}{4}$, $\frac{3}{4}$, $-\frac{3}{4}$, $\frac{4}{3}$, $-\frac{4}{3}$, ...

(How does this continue?)

Infinite sets may be cardinally equivalent to a subset. With finite sets this is not possible.

1.17 | Are there infinite sets that are not countable?

Consider A = set of the points of a particular interval (e.g., the set of the real numbers x for which $0 \leq x \leq 1$).

A cannot be counted. Suppose that A could be counted. Then we could number the points of A:

$$a_1, a_2, a_3, \ldots$$

On A we can choose a sub-interval A_1 such that

$$a_1 \notin A_1. \tag{1}$$

(Intervals are conceived as including their terminal points.) On A_1 we choose a sub-interval A_2 such that $a_2 \notin A_2$. And so on. In general (for all natural n): on A_n we choose a sub-interval A_{n+1} such that

$$a_{n+1} \notin A_{n+1}. \tag{2}$$

The lengths $A_1, A_2, \ldots$ constitute a decreasing series (also called: nested sets) $A_1 \supset A_2 \supset A_3 \supset \ldots.$ Let c be a point common to all of them. Hence

$$c \in A_n \quad \text{for all} \quad n. \tag{3}$$

$c \in A$; hence, c must have been given a number. Let this be p. Then

$$c = a_p. \tag{4}$$

But

$$a_p \notin A_p,$$

whereas from (3) and (4) it follows that

$$a_p \in A_p.$$

This is a contradiction. Our assumption must therefore have been wrong. Hence there is no way of counting A. A is infinite, but not countably infinite.

Note that we have here made use of the "intuitive" notion that an infinite number of nested intervals have a point in common.

1.18 | When can A be said to be cardinally majorized by B? In the example of the people and chairs we said that there were fewer people than chairs if chairs remained vacant when all the people had sat down. In dealing with infinite sets this sort of test is not enough, however. For example, the set of the natural numbers can be mapped 1–1 into itself in such a manner that nothing remains and also in such a manner that there is a remainder (take the mapping f defined by $f(x) = x$ or the mapping g defined by $g(x) = 2x$). Hence we define:

A is called *cardinally majorized* by *B* if there exists a 1–1 mapping of *A* into *B*, but no 1–1 mapping of *B* into *A*. *B* is said to be *cardinally minorized* by *A*.

We may also say: *A* is called cardinally majorized by *B* if *A* is cardinally equivalent to a part of *B*, but *B* is not cardinally equivalent to a part of *A*.

Example: The set *A* of points of the interval (see 1.17) is cardinally minorized by that of the natural numbers, *N*. Indeed by successively numbering an infinite number of points $a_1, a_2, \ldots$ of *A* we find a portion of *A* which is cardinally equivalent to *N*, whereas it is immediately apparent from 1.17 that *A* cannot be cardinally equivalent to any part of *N*.

1.19 | In 1.4 it was shown that a set with *n* members has 2^n subsets, hence, certainly more than *n*.

We now take an arbitrary (possibly an infinite) set *A* and form the set Ω of all subsets of *A*, i.e.,

$$X \in \Omega \quad \text{if, and only if,} \quad X \subset A.$$

We shall show that Ω cardinally majorizes *A*.

THEOREM: *The set of the subsets of A cardinally majorizes A.*

Proof*): We assign to each $a \in A$ the subset (a) of *A* which consists only of the member *a*; this is a 1–1 mapping of *A* onto a part of Ω. We must now show: there is *no* 1–1 mapping of Ω onto a part of *A*. Or in other words: there is no 1–1 mapping of a part A_0 of *A* onto Ω. Even the following is true.

There exists no mapping of a part A_0 of *A* onto Ω.

To prove this I assume: let *f* be a mapping of $A_0 \subset A$ onto Ω. From this I shall prove a contradiction.

With every $x, f(x)$ is a member of Ω, and therefore a part of *A*. There is sense in asking

$$\text{whether} \quad x \in f(x) \quad \text{or} \quad x \notin f(x).$$

Let the set of the $x \in A_0$ with $x \notin f(x)$ be denoted by *U*. Hence

$$x \in U, \text{ if and only if, } x \in A_0, \text{ and } x \notin f(x). \tag{1}$$

Of course $U \subset A$, hence $U \in \Omega$. As *f* maps A_0 *onto* Ω, there is a *u* with

$$u \in A_0 \tag{2}$$

and

$$U = f(u). \tag{3}$$

*) This proof makes rather high demands upon the reader's capacity for abstract thought. It can be skipped in the first perusal of the book.

Which is true now

$u \in U$ or $u \notin U$?

We have to verify this in (1). Insert u for x. Then (1) says:

$u \in U$, if and only if $u \in A_0$ and $u \notin f(u)$.   (4)

According to (2) $u \in A_0$ any way, so we can omit this extra condition in (4):

$u \in U$, if and only if, $u \notin f(u)$.   (5)

Taking (3) into account, we then have

$u \in f(u)$, if and only if, $u \notin f(u)$.   (6)

This is the desired contradiction, and hence the theorem is proved. From this theorem it follows, that for every set A, there exists a set B, so that A cardinally minorizes B.

1.20 | With two sets A and B one of the alternatives α and α' must apply:
α) A is cardinally equivalent to a part of B, or
α') A is not cardinally equivalent to a part of B.
Furthermore:
β) B is cardinally equivalent to a part of A, or
β') B is not cardinally equivalent to a part of A.
From these alternatives it is possible to form four combinations:
α and β': then, as per definition, A cardinally minorizes B.
α' and β: then, as per definition, B cardinally minorizes A.
α and β: then A and B are cardinally equivalent. This is known as BERNSTEIN's equivalence theorem. Its proof is by no means easy and will therefore be omitted.
α' and β': this case cannot occur. The proof of this will likewise be omitted. It is based on what is known as ZERMELO's postulate of choice.
If we accept these assertions, then it follows that:

Two sets A and B will always be in one of the three states: A and B are cardinally equivalent, A cardinally majorizes B, B cardinally majorizes A.

1.21 | We have stated when two sets are cardinally equivalent (and when one of them cardinally majorizes the other), but we did not speak of the *cardinal number* of a set. For finite sets we might define, the cardinal number of a set A as the number of elements of A. For infinite sets, however, this is not a satisfactory definition.
In the early stages of development of set theory the definition given was: the

cardinal number of a set A is that which is common to all sets that are cardinally equivalent to A.

The phrase "that which is common to" is very vague. Nowadays one has a different recipe for such definitions. To explain this, let us consider another example.

If we wish to ascertain whether a particular body A weighs one pound, we compare it with a standard weight of one pound by means of a balance. In more general terms, if we wish to determine the weight of a body A, we compare this body with standard weights. We try to find a standard weight that is just as heavy. If we succeed in this, we assign to A that standard weight as its weight.

Quite apart from a set of standard weights we can, in any particular case, ascertain with the aid of a balance whether or not two bodies A and B are equally heavy. To all bodies that are just as heavy as A we shall assign the same weight. We shall lump all these bodies together into one class*) which will be designated by $\{A\}$. All $X \in \{A\}$ are just as heavy as A. They constitute one weight class which differs from other weight classes. To all bodies belonging to the same weight class we wish to assign the same weight. The weight of A is therefore dependent only upon the class $\{A\}$ of which A is a member, and for members of different classes the weight must accordingly be different.

Well, the simplest distinctive feature of bodies, which depends on their weight class only and which is different for each weight class, is the weight class itself to which the bodies respectively belong. Hence it is reasonable to define by the weight of a body the weight class of which it is a member. Or: by the weight of the body A we understand the class of all bodies that are just as heavy as A.

Similarly: the *cardinal number* of a set A is the class of all sets that are cardinally equivalent to A.

1.22 | There is still a gap in the foregoing. Let us write for "A is just as heavy as B": $A \sim B$.

The weight class $\{A\}$ of A was defined by:

(0)　　$X \in \{A\}$ if, and only if, $X \sim A$.

Of course we wish every body to be a member of a weight class and more particularly that A should be a member of $\{A\}$; hence

(1)　　$A \in \{A\}$.

---

*) "Class" is a synonym for "set" and is used in order to avoid too much repetition of the latter word.

Furthermore, we want a weight class to be characterized by each of its members, i.e.,

(2)　　if $B \in \{A\}$,　then　$\{A\} = \{B\}$.

But if, in addition to (1), we only require that

(2′)　　if $B \in \{A\}$,　then　$\{A\} \subset \{B\}$,

then (2) will be automatically satisfied, for then we can reason as follows: if $B \in \{A\}$, then $\{A\} \subset \{B\}$; hence because of (1): $A \in \{B\}$; therefore because of (2′) (but now with interchanging of A and B): $\{B\} \subset \{A\}$; hence $\{A\} = \{B\}$. Now, according to definition (0), assertion (1) is the same as

(1*)　$A \sim A$

and (2′) is the same as

(2*)　　if $B \sim A$　and　$C \sim A$,　then　$C \sim B$.

From (1*) and (2*) also follows

(3*)　　if $A \sim B$,　then　$B \sim A$,

as we see on replacing B by A, A by B and C by B in (2*).

(1*), (2*), (3*) are evidently true if one reads the sign "$\sim$" as "equally heavy". But they are also true if we take "$\sim$" to signify "equally long", "equally old", "equally expensive", "equally beautiful", "congruent", "similar to", "equal to", "simultaneous with". A more neutral reading of the sign "$\sim$" is *equivalent to*.

Expressed in words, the three laws (1*), (2*), (3*) will then be:

(1″)　Every object is equivalent to itself (*reflexivity*).
(2″)　If two objects are equivalent to a third, then they are also mutually equivalent (*transitivity*).
(3″)　If an object is equivalent to a second object, then the second object is also equivalent to the first (*symmetry*).

Relations (such as "being equally heavy", "being congruent", etc.) that possess the properties (1″), (2″) and (3″) — actually, the first two properties are sufficient — are known as *equivalence relations*.

If, in a set Ω, an equivalence relation is given, i.e., if we know of each pair of members A and B of Ω whether $A \sim B$ holds true or not, then we can subdivide the whole Ω into classes by putting mutually equivalent members of Ω into the same class. The equivalence class $\{A\}$ is then defined as the set of all $X \in \Omega$ with $X \sim A$.

The concept of "cardinal equivalence" is likewise an equivalence concept. Indeed in the first place: every set is cardinally equivalent to itself, namely, through the identity mapping.

Secondly: if B and C are cardinally equivalent to A, then there are 1–1 mappings f of B onto A and g of C onto A; if h is the inverse of f, then hg, as a combination of "1–1 mappings onto", will also be a "1–1 mapping onto"; hence C is cardinally equivalent to B.

The cardinal equivalence class of a set A is also referred to as the *cardinal number* of A.

1.23 | Between pairs of bodies there exists also the relation of "being less heavy" (or "being heavier"). This relation can also be transferred to the pairs of weight classes, if the following is known:

If A and A' are equally heavy, and also B and B', and if A is less heavy than B, then A' is also less heavy than B'.

Whether A is less heavy than B, then only depends on the classes of which A and B are members.

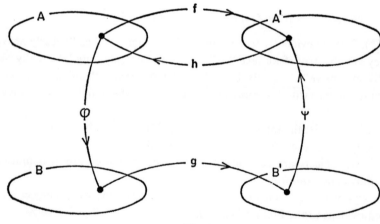

Fig. 3

Something similar applies to the cardinals. If A is cardinally equivalent to A', and B to B', and if A cardinally minorizes B, then A' must cardinally minorize B'. Indeed then there are 1–1 mappings

f of A onto A',
g of B onto B',
φ of A into B,

and there is

no 1–1 mapping of B into A.

Now if h is the inverse of f, then there is the 1–1 mapping

$g\varphi h$ of A' into B',

and if furthermore there was a 1–1 mapping

ψ of B' into A',

then

$h\psi g$, being then a 1–1 mapping of B into A,

would be contradictory to the presupposition.

Hence we can define: if A cardinally minorizes B, then the cardinal number of A is said to be *smaller* than that of B.

1.24 | With this concept of "smaller" the cardinal numbers form what is called an ordered set. Just as, for example, the natural numbers or the real numbers. A set Z is said to be *ordered* by means of a relation "$<$" (read "smaller than") if, for every two different members a, b of Z, one and only one of the two possibilities

$a < b$ or $b < a$

occurs, and if, for every three different members a, b, c, of Z it follows

from $a < b$ and $b < c$, that $a < c$

(transitivity of the $<$-relation).

Instead of $a < b$ we also write $b > a$; instead of "$a < b$ or $a = b$" we write $a \leq b$; and instead of $a \leq b$ also $b \geq a$.

Pairs

1.25 | The forming of classes by means of an equivalence notion is one of the commonest methods of forming mathematical concepts. Here are a few more examples.

Starting from the integers, the rational numbers can be defined as fractions of integers. Doing this it is obvious that $\frac{8}{10}$ and $\frac{12}{15}$ must represent the same rational number. This can be formulated more exactly as follows: By

$\ulcorner a, b \urcorner$

we mean the pair formed from a and b and more particularly, the *directed pair* i.e., $\ulcorner a, b\urcorner$ is different from $\ulcorner b, a\urcorner$ (at any rate if $a \neq b$). (Hence $\ulcorner a, b\urcorner$ is not merely the set with members a and b.)

Given two sets A, B, we can form the set of all pairs $\ulcorner a, b\urcorner$ with $a \in A$ and $b \in B$. We shall call this $\ulcorner A, B\urcorner$. Hence

$$c \in \ulcorner A, B\urcorner \text{ if, and only if, } c = \ulcorner a, b\urcorner \text{ for certain } a \in A \text{ and } b \in B.$$

Let G be the set of all integers and let H be the set of all integers $\neq 0$. We shall form $\ulcorner G, H\urcorner$ — i.e., the set of all $\ulcorner a, b\urcorner$ with $a \in G$ and $b \in H$ — and remember at the back of our minds that $\ulcorner a, b\urcorner$ should actually represent the fraction $\frac{a}{b}$. Hence we introduce an equivalence relation: for

$$\ulcorner a, b\urcorner \in \ulcorner G, H\urcorner \quad \text{and} \quad \ulcorner a', b'\urcorner \in \ulcorner G, H\urcorner$$

we put

$$\ulcorner a, b\urcorner \sim \ulcorner a', b'\urcorner$$

if, and only if,

$$ab' = a'b.$$

(Think of the fractions $\frac{8}{10}$ and $\frac{12}{15}$; they represent the same rational number because $8 \times 15 = 12 \times 10$.) Verify that this is an equivalence relation as envisaged in 1.22, (1*)–(2*), and form by means of this equivalence, the division into classes.

The class of which $\ulcorner a, b\urcorner$ is a member, *viz.*,

$$\{\ulcorner a, b\urcorner\},$$

is called a rational number. (Thus, for example, $\ulcorner 4, 5\urcorner, \ulcorner -4, -5\urcorner, \ulcorner -8, -10\urcorner,$ $\ulcorner 80, 100\urcorner$ are in the same class — the rational number that is normally represented by the fraction $\frac{4}{5}$.)

We can now define the addition of rational numbers by beginning with the addition of directed pairs. We define:

$$\text{if} \quad \ulcorner a, b\urcorner \in \ulcorner G, H\urcorner \quad \text{and} \quad \ulcorner c, d\urcorner \in \ulcorner G, H\urcorner,$$
$$\text{then} \quad \ulcorner a, b\urcorner + \ulcorner c, d\urcorner = \ulcorner ad + bc, bd\urcorner.$$

This is again $\in \ulcorner G, H\urcorner$ because $b \neq 0$, $d \neq 0$, hence $bd \neq 0$.

(Verify that this corresponds to the ordinary addition rule for fractions.)

If each summand is replaced by an equivalent one, the sum is likewise replaced by an equivalent one. For let

$$\ulcorner a, b\urcorner \sim \ulcorner a', b'\urcorner, \quad \ulcorner c, d\urcorner \sim \ulcorner c', d'\urcorner,$$

then

$$ab' = a'b, \quad cd' = c'd.$$ (*)

We must show that

$$\ulcorner ad + bc, bd \urcorner \sim \ulcorner a'd' + b'c', b'd' \urcorner,$$

and therefore that

$$(ad + bc)b'd' = (a'd' + b'c')bd.$$ (**)

Now the left-hand member of (**) is

$$= adb'd' + bcb'd' = ab'dd' + bb'cd'$$

and because of (*)

$$= a'bdd' + bb'c'd = (a'd' + b'c')bd,$$

and this is equal to the right-hand member of (**).
Now for two rational numbers we can uniquely define the sum

$$\{\ulcorner a, b \urcorner\} + \{\ulcorner c, d \urcorner\} = \{\ulcorner ad + bc, bd \urcorner\},$$

because we have shown that the class of the sum of two pairs is not dependent upon the choice of those pairs in their class.
Similarly we define the other operations with rational numbers and prove the various well known arithmetical laws.

1.26 | Another example of the forming of classes by means of an equivalence relation:
Let G again represent the set of integers.
Let m be a fixed integer. Let H be the set of m-folds, i.e.,

$$c \in H \text{ if and only if } c = md \text{ for certain } d \in G.$$

One easily sees that, if $b \in H$ and $c \in H$, also $c - b \in H$.
We now put

$$a \sim b \text{ if and only if } a - b \in H,$$

i.e., if the difference $a - b$ is an m-fold.
This is a proper equivalence relation, for:

$$a \sim a \text{ because } a - a = 0 \in H;$$

if $\quad b \sim a \text{ and } c \sim a,$

then $b - a \in H$ and $c - a \in H$,
therefore $(b - a) - (c - a) \in H$,
hence $c - b \in H$,
hence $c \sim b$.

The class $\{a\}$ consists of all integers which differ from a by an m-fold. The transition from a to $\{a\}$ means that we ignore multiples of m.

For example, this is what a clock does (for $m = 12$) in identifying 12 o'clock, 13 o'clock, etc. with 0 o'clock, 1 o'clock, etc.; or a calculating machine with six positions in the counting mechanism ($m = 1,000,000$) which gives for $334,896 + 884,391$, the answer: $219,287$.

The classes $\{a\}$ as defined just now are also called: integers modulo m. The operations of addition, subtraction and multiplication between such classes can be defined by:

$$\{a\} + \{b\} = \{a + b\},$$
$$\{a\} - \{b\} = \{a - b\},$$
$$\{a\} \cdot \{b\} = \{a \cdot b\}.$$

Here again we must show that

if $a' \sim a$, $b' \sim b$, then $a' + b' \sim a + b$, etc.

The reader may do this for himself.

Example: Modulo 12 is $\{7\} + \{8\} = \{3\}$, $\{7\} - \{8\} = \{11\}$, $\{7\} \cdot \{8\} = \{8\}$, $\{3\} \cdot \{4\} = \{0\}$.

The last formula shows that modulo 12 a product may be $\{0\}$, although none of the factors is $\{0\}$. Consequently modulo 12 division does not work.

Modulo 7 we can divide in the same way as is done in the set of rational numbers. There, every $\{a\} \neq \{0\}$ has an inverse: $\{1\} = \{1\} \cdot \{1\} = \{2\} \cdot \{4\} = \{3\} \cdot \{5\} = \{6\} \cdot \{6\}$; hence, for example, $\{4\}$ is the inverse of $\{2\}$.

The same holds modulo every prime number m (number $\neq 0$ and $\neq 1$ which has no divisors other than $1, -1, m, -m$).

1.27 | Set theory is a modern field of mathematics. Its founder was GEORG CANTOR (1845–1918).

2 | PROPOSITIONS

2.1 | In logic we understand by "proposition" what in linguistic terms is represented by a meaningful assertive sentence.

For example: All people are mortal.

Or: Socrates is a man.
Or: If $a < b$, then $b > a$.
Or: All negroes are white.
Or: All white men are white.
Or: If snow burns, ash remains.

Propositions need not be true statements.
"Proposition" is not the same thing as "sentence". "Sentence" is a linguistic concept, whereas "proposition" is a logic concept. "Socrates is a man" and "Socrate est un homme" relate to the same proposition, but in different languages.
"What is the time?" and "Stop it!" do not relate to propositions. On the other hand, the following statements do: "John asked Peter what time it was" and "John said to Peter: 'stop it!' "

2.2 | In Chapter 3 we shall further analyse simple sentences such as "Socrates is a man", corresponding to grammatical analysis. In the present chapter we shall break down propositions only in so far as the constituents thereof are also propositions.
To join sentences into more elaborate ones we use connectives.

Joining by means of "and":
Sweden won from Germany *and* Brazil won from Sweden.

Joining by means of "or":
The bell is out of order *or* the people are not at home.

Joining by means of "if ... then":
If a train is coming, *then* the signal is at danger.

Joining by means of "if and only if":
If and only if a train is coming, the signal is at danger.

Multiple joining occurs in:
If A wins from *B and C* wins from *D, then A* will play against *C and B* will play against *D.*

There are, of course, many more connectives, but those mentioned above are of particular interest to us because of their specifically logical character.

In order to ascertain whether a composite proposition "*p* and *q*" is true, we need merely know whether the two components *p*, *q* are true. If so, then "*p* and *q*" is true. It is, for this, not necessary to have any further knowledge of the content of *p* or of *q*. Also, we can infer the truth of "*p* or *q*" if we know that at least one of the component propositions is true; the actual content of *p* and of *q* does not matter.

Note: "*p* or *q*" is considered to be true also if both *p* and *q* are true.

Something similar is applicable to "if *p*, then *q*". When is such a proposition true? Let us consider one of the examples given above. There are four possibilities, represented by the four cases in the following scheme:

	train coming	not coming
signal danger		
safe		

Which of these four possibilities confirm the statement

"if a train is coming, then the signal is at danger",

and which of them contradict it? If we find a train coming and the signal at danger (top left-hand case), the statement is confirmed; also, if there is no train and the signal at clear (bottom right-hand case). And this is still true if there is no train and the signal is at danger (top right-hand case), inasmuch as the statement says nothing about what happens if there is no train: the signal may than be at clear or at danger. But if it ever should occur that we find a train coming and yet find the signal to be at clear (bottom left-hand case), then the statement will have been refuted.

We thus find: A proposition "if *p*, then *q*" is untrue only if *p* is true and *q* is nevertheless untrue; in all other cases it is true — i.e., it is true both if *p* is untrue and *q* is arbitrary and also if *q* is true and *p* is arbitrary.

Henceforth we shall employ the following notation:

$p \wedge q$ for "*p* and *q*",
$p \vee q$ for "*p* or *q*",
$p \rightarrow q$ for "if *p*, then *q*",
$p \leftrightarrow q$ for "*p* if, and only if *q*".

The symbol $\vee$ is derived from the "v" of the Latin "vel" (meaning "or"); the $\wedge$ is the $\vee$ upside down. The symbols $\rightarrow$ and $\leftrightarrow$ are self-evident.

The various connectives have their own special names:

$p \wedge q$ conjunction (of p and q),
$p \vee q$ disjunction (of p and q),
$p \rightarrow q$ implication (of p to q),
$p \leftrightarrow q$ mutual implication.

In $p \rightarrow q$ the terms "antecedent" and "consequent" are used to denote p and q respectively.

In addition to the connectives $\wedge$, $\vee$, $\rightarrow$, $\leftrightarrow$, which always make two propositions into one new one, the connective "$\neg$" is of importance, which should be read as "not". This connective turns a proposition p into a proposition $\neg p$ (= not-p). "$\neg$ (there is a train coming)" means "there is no train coming". In order to know whether $\neg p$ is true, we need only know whether p is true; if p is true, then $\neg p$ is untrue, and if p is untrue, then $\neg p$ is true. The junction formed by means of the connective "$\neg$" is known as the

$\neg p$, negation (of p).

2.3 | The calculus of propositions can now be described as follows. From given propositions $p, q, r, \ldots$ we can, with the aid of the connectives, construct new propositions, e.g.

$$(\neg p \wedge r) \rightarrow [(p \rightarrow q) \vee (\neg q \rightarrow \neg p)].$$

Of course, we must pay attention to the sequence of construction and, if necessary, we designate this by means of parentheses. Thus

$$(p \vee q) \wedge r \quad \text{and} \quad p \vee (q \wedge r)$$

differ as follows: in the former case we first form $p \vee q$ and connect the result by means of $\wedge$ with r; in the latter case we first form $q \wedge r$ and then connect it with p by means of $\vee$.

With regard to $\neg$ the following convention will be adopted: if $\neg$ is followed by a letter, it relates to that letter; if $\neg$ is followed by an opening parenthesis, it relates to the whole expression up to the corresponding closing parenthesis. Hence in

$$\neg p \vee r$$

we first form the negation of p and then combine it with r by disjunction, whereas in

$$\neg(p \vee r),$$

$p \vee r$ is formed first and then negated.

What is of particular interest to us in propositions is their *truth value*, i.e., whether they are true or false. To ascertain this, we need not have an information about the separate component propositions other than *their* truth values. These completely determine the truth value of the compound proposition.

We shall use the symbol

0 for false, and
1 for true.

Furthermore, the truth value of a proposition will be designated by $|p|$. Hence for any particular p it holds that $|p| = 0$ or $|p| = 1$.

For each connective we can draw up a truth table showing when a combination formed by means of that connective is true and when it is false.

p	q	$\neg p$	$p \wedge q$	$p \vee q$	$p \to q$	$p \leftrightarrow q$	p / q
0	0	1	0	0	1	1	1
0	1	1	0	1	1	0	0
1	0	0	0	1	0	0	0
1	1	0	1	1	1	1	0

On the left of the vertical line are indicated all four possibilities that may happen with the pair p, q (i.e., "p false" and "p true" combined with "q false" and "q true"). To the right of the vertical line are indicated the values that the derived propositions will then have. For example, $|p \wedge q| = 1$ if and only if $|p| = 1$ and $|q| = 1$; $p \to q$ is false if, and only if, p is true and q is nevertheless false; etc. In the above scheme is a new connective, which is theoretically rather important, the "bar" in p / q, which is to be read as

p / q, neither p nor q.

In fact this is true only if both p and q are false.

Now we can determine the truth values of more complex combinations and draw up truthtables for them.

When is $\neg p \vee q$ true? Or alternatively: when is it false?

Only if $\neg p$ is false and q is also false. We can express this as follows: only if p is true and q is false.

It thus appears that $\neg p \vee q$ is true and false under precisely the same conditions as $p \to q$. Hence $\neg p \vee q$ and $p \to q$ are said to be *equivalent*,

$|\neg p \vee q| = |p \to q|$ for all p, q.

Another example: $\neg(\neg p \wedge \neg q)$ is false if and only if $\neg p \wedge \neg q$ is true. This

is precisely so if $\neg p$ is true and also $\neg q$ is true, which will be the case if p is false and q is false. But $p \lor q$ is also false only under these conditions. Hence $\neg(\neg p \land \neg q)$ and $p \lor q$ are equivalent.
Hence

$$|\neg(\neg p \land \neg q)| = |p \lor q| \quad \text{for all } p, q.$$

Other evident cases of equivalence are

$$|\neg(\neg p)| = |p| \quad \text{for all } p,$$
$$|p \land q| = |q \land p| \text{ for all } p, q.$$

We can ascertain whether two propositions are equivalent by systematically substituting 0 and 1 for the letters occurring therein and working it out according to the truth tables.

Example:

p	q	r	$\neg[(p \lor q) \land r]$	$r \to (\neg p \land \neg q)$	$(r \to \neg p) \land \neg q$
0	0	0	1	1	1
0	0	1	1	1	1
0	1	0	1	1	0
0	1	1	0	0	0
1	0	0	1	1	1
1	0	1	0	0	0
1	1	0	1	1	0
1	1	1	0	0	0

2.4 | The compound propositions

$$p \to p, \; p \lor \neg p, \; (p \to q) \to (\neg q \to \neg p),$$
$$\neg(p \lor q) \leftrightarrow (\neg p \land \neg q), \; p \to (q \to p),$$
$$(p \to q) \to ((q \to r) \to (p \to r))$$

exhibit the particular feature that they are *always true*, i.e. irrespective as to whether the component propositions $p, q, r, \ldots$ are true or false. (Verify this.) On the other hand,

$$p \land \neg p, \; (p \to q) \land (\neg q \land p),$$
$$[(p \to q) \land (q \to r)] \land (p \land \neg r)$$

are always false, i.e., irrespective as to whether $p, q, r, \ldots$ are true or false. (Verify this.)

The propositions

$$p, \; p \vee p, \; p \wedge p$$

are sometimes true and sometimes false (namely, true if p is true, and false if p is false).

$$(p \rightarrow q) \rightarrow (q \rightarrow p)$$

is also sometimes true and sometimes false (namely, false if p is false and q is true, and true in all other cases). Also

$$(p \rightarrow q) \rightarrow (r \rightarrow q)$$

is sometimes true and sometimes false.

Given a proposition A composed of propositions $p, q, r, \ldots$ we can try to assign to $p, q, r, \ldots$ such truth values that A becomes true. This is called "satisfying" the proposition A. If we can succeed in doing this, we shall call A *satisfiable*. (If it is not possible to satisfy A, then A is always false.)

We can do the same if a whole set Ω of propositions A is given. If we can assign to $p, q, r \ldots$ such truth values that all $A \in \Omega$ simultaneously become true, then Ω is called satisfiable.

We can also try to assign to $p, q, r, \ldots$ such truth values that A becomes false. If we succeed in doing this, then A is called *disputable*. (If we fail in doing this, then A is true for any valuation $p, q, r, \ldots$, i.e., A is always true.)

A set Ω of propositions is said to be disputable if, for an appropriate valuation of $p, q, r, \ldots$, at least one $A \in \Omega$ becomes false.

From the foregoing it follows that: For a proposition A "not satisfiable" is the same as "always false". Similarly, "not disputable" is the same as "always true". If A is always true, then A is also satisfiable. If A is always false, then A is also disputable. If A is always true, then $\neg A$ is always false. If A is always false, then $\neg A$ is always true. If A is satisfiable, then $\neg A$ is disputable. If A is disputable, then $\neg A$ is satisfiable.

2.5 | *The Equivalence Principle*

In 2.3 we were introduced to equivalent propositions, e.g.,

$$p \rightarrow q \quad \text{and} \quad \neg p \vee q,$$
$$\neg(\neg p \wedge \neg q) \quad \text{and} \quad p \vee q,$$
$$\neg(\neg p) \quad \text{and} \quad p.$$

From these pairs we can obtain propositions that are always true, namely

$$(p \to q) \leftrightarrow (\neg p \lor q),$$
$$\neg(\neg p \land \neg q) \leftrightarrow (p \lor q),$$
$$\neg(\neg p) \leftrightarrow p.$$

This is because, for

$$A \leftrightarrow B$$

to be true, it is necessary that A and B are always simultaneously true and false, and this is precisely the case with propositions of equivalent value. This is stated in general by the

Equivalence principle: If A and B are composed of $p, q, r,\ldots$ and if they are equivalent, i.e., if

$$|A| = |B| \quad \text{for all } p, q, r, \ldots,$$

then

$$A \leftrightarrow B$$

is always true — and conversely: if $A \leftrightarrow B$ is always true, then A and B are equivalent.

2.6 | The Deduction Principle

Another method of arriving at propositions that are always true is based on the principle of deduction.

$p \to q$ is certainly not always true (it is false if p is true and q is false). However, if we suppose q to be true, then $p \to q$ is also true because then the case where $p \to q$ was false will precisely not occur. Hence: on the assumption "q is true", $p \to q$ is also true. But from this follows a formula that is always true, namely

$$q \to (p \to q).$$

The method supplied here can be formulated in general terms as follows:

Deduction principle: Let $A_1, \ldots, A_n, A, B$ be propositions composed of $p, q, r, \ldots$ Suppose that B is true for all valuations of $p, q, r, \ldots$ for which $A_1, \ldots, A_n, A$ together are true. Then

$$A \to B$$

is true for all valuations of $p, q, r, \ldots$ for which $A_1, \ldots, A_n$ together are true.

For suppose there was a valuation of $p, q, r, \ldots$ which made $A_1, \ldots, A_n$ true but $A \rightarrow B$ false. Hence, for this evaluation $A_1, \ldots, A_n$, A would be true and nevertheless B would be false, which is contradictory to the assumption.

More briefly the deduction principle can be stated as follows:

If B is true on the assumption that $A_1, \ldots, A_n$, A together are true, then $A \rightarrow B$ is true on the assumption that $A_1, \ldots, A_n$ together are true.

More particularly:

If B is true on the assumption that A is true, then $A \rightarrow B$ is always true.

Example:

$$[(p \rightarrow q) \wedge (q \rightarrow r)] \rightarrow (p \rightarrow r)$$

is always true.

This can be shown as follows. Suppose: $(p \rightarrow q) \wedge (q \rightarrow r)$. We wish to prove: $p \rightarrow r$. (If we succeed in doing this, then, according to the deduction principle, we are ready.) From the assumption it appears that $p \rightarrow q$ and also that $q \rightarrow r$ is true (for only then that conjunction is true).

Now suppose also that p is true. Then, because $p \rightarrow q$ is true, q must also be true (see the truth table of the implication). From "q is true" it likewise follows, since $q \rightarrow r$ is true, that r is true.

Hence, on the assumption "$(p \rightarrow q) \wedge (q \rightarrow r)$ is true" and "p is true", we find that r is true. According to the deduction principle therefore:

$p \rightarrow r$ is true on the assumption that $(p \rightarrow q) \wedge (q \rightarrow r)$ is true,

and from this it follows — as already indicated — that

$$[(p \rightarrow q) \wedge (q \rightarrow r)] \rightarrow (p \rightarrow r)$$

is always true.

By means of this method prove that

$$(p \rightarrow q) \rightarrow [(q \rightarrow r) \rightarrow (p \rightarrow r)],$$
$$[(p \rightarrow q) \wedge (r \rightarrow s)] \rightarrow [(p \wedge r) \rightarrow (q \wedge s)],$$
$$[(p \rightarrow q) \vee (r \rightarrow s)] \rightarrow [(p \wedge r) \rightarrow (q \vee s)],$$

are always true.

Use the equivalence and deduction principles to show that

$$[p \rightarrow (q \rightarrow r)] \leftrightarrow [(p \wedge q) \rightarrow r]$$

is always true — i.e., prove by means of the deduction principle that

$$[p \rightarrow (q \rightarrow r)] \rightarrow [(p \wedge q) \rightarrow r]$$

and

$$[(p \wedge q) \rightarrow r] \rightarrow [p \rightarrow (q \rightarrow r)]$$

are always true.

A variant of the principle of deduction is the principle of disjunction, which the reader may already have applied unconsciously in studying the foregoing problems. In the course of a proof it may occur that we distinguish certain cases α and β and then draw the same inference D both from α and from β, finally concluding that D holds true in any case.
This is the

Disjunction principle: Let $A_1, \ldots, A_n, B, C, D$ be propositions composed of $p, q, r, \ldots$. Suppose that for any valuation of $p, q, r, \ldots$, for which $A_1, \ldots, A_n$ are true, either B or C is true. Suppose moreover that D is true on the assumption "$A_1, \ldots, A_n, B$ true" and also on the assumption "$A_1, \ldots, A_n, C$ true". Then D is true on the assumption "$A_1, \ldots, A_n$ true".

The deduction and disjunction principles could also have been formulated for a — possibly infinite — system of propositions instead of the n propositions $A_1, \ldots, A_n$.

2.7 | *The Principle of Negation*

Principle of negation: If A is always true, then $\neg A$ is always false. This follows from 2.4 (end).
$p \wedge \neg p$ is always false, as appears from the truth table. (p and not-p cannot exist simultaneously — they are mutually exclusive: the law of *contradiction*.)
Hence

$$\neg(p \wedge \neg p)$$

is always true.
Still more principles of this kind can be formulated.

2.8 | *The Principle of Substitution*

Principle of substitution: Let A be a proposition that is always true, composed

of $p, q, r,\ldots$. Any proposition derived from A by substituting propositions for $p, q, r,\ldots$ is also always true.
This is obvious.

Example: $q \rightarrow (p \rightarrow q)$ is a known proposition that is always true. We substitute $p \rightarrow q$ for q and $\neg(r \vee p)$ for p. Then we obtain the following proposition which is always true

$$(p \rightarrow q) \rightarrow \{[\neg(r \vee p)] \rightarrow (p \rightarrow q)\}.$$

2.9 | The Modus Ponens

All the foregoing principles serve the purpose of deriving new propositions from certain always-true propositions. We thus obtain longer and longer always-true propositions. Now we will learn a principle by means of which always-true propositions can be reduced to shorter ones.

Modus ponens: If A is always true and if $A \rightarrow B$ is always true, then B is also always true.
Scheme:

$$A$$
$$\frac{A \rightarrow B}{B}.$$

In fact if any value is assigned to the $p, q, r, \ldots$ of which A and B are composed, then — according to the truth table of the implication and since $A \rightarrow B$ is true — only the following cases can occur:

A false and B true, A false and B false, A true and B true.

Here all cases with "A false" are ruled out (for A is always true), so that only the third case remains, and in that case B is true.

Example: We know the always-true proposition

$$p \rightarrow (q \rightarrow p).$$

Now replace p by any particular always-true proposition A (principle of substitution);

$$A \rightarrow (q \rightarrow A)$$

will then always be true. But because A is always true, then

$$q \rightarrow A$$

is always true, according to the modus ponens. Thus, for example, the following is always true:

$$q \rightarrow [p \rightarrow (q \rightarrow p)]$$

2.10 | A List

We can draw up a list of propositions that are always true. Verify the truth by compiling truth tables or by means of the principles discussed in the foregoing.

(1) $(p \leftrightarrow q) \leftrightarrow [(p \rightarrow q) \wedge (q \rightarrow p)]$.
(2) $(p \leftrightarrow q) \leftrightarrow (q \leftrightarrow p)$.
(3) $(p \leftrightarrow q) \rightarrow (p \rightarrow q)$.
(4) $p \leftrightarrow p$.
(5) $\neg(p \wedge \neg p)$.

(See 2.7, the law of *contradiction*.)

(6) $(p \wedge \neg p) \rightarrow q$.

(On the assumption of a contradiction everything is true.)

(7) $\neg\neg p \leftrightarrow p$.

(The law of the *double negation*.)

(8) $p \vee \neg p$.

(The law of the *excluded middle*: p or not-p — there is no third possibility.)

(9) $(p \wedge p) \leftrightarrow p$.
(10) $(p \vee p) \leftrightarrow p$.
(11) $p \rightarrow (q \rightarrow p)$.

(See 2.6. If p is true, then p is true on any assumption.)

(12) $[p \rightarrow (q \rightarrow r)] \leftrightarrow [(p \wedge q) \rightarrow r]$.

(See 2.6.)

(13) $\neg p \rightarrow (p \rightarrow q)$.

(Can be obtained from (12) on substitution of $\neg p$ for p, p for q, q for r, having due regard to (6).

(14) $(p \rightarrow q) \vee (q \rightarrow p)$.

(A remarkable formula. Follows directly from the truth table of the implication.

If p is true, then the second member of the disjunction is true; if p is false, then the first member is true; hence at least one member of the disjunction is true.)

(15) $(p \to q) \leftrightarrow (\neg p \lor q)$.

(16) $(p \to q) \leftrightarrow (\neg q \to \neg p)$.

(The law of *contraposition*. On this is based the indirect proof or *reductio ad absurdum*. We wish to prove that q is true on the assumption p. According to the principle of deduction this comes to a proof of $p \to q$. Instead of this we may, according to (16), also prove $\neg q \to \neg p$. Hence: snppose $\neg q$, i.e., q is false, and from this assumption derive $\neg p$. We thus obtain $p \to q$ via $\neg q \to \neg p$.)

(17) $[(p \to q) \land (q \to r)] \to (p \to r)$.

(See 2.6. The *transitivity of the implication*.)

(18) $(p \to q) \to [(q \to r) \to (p \to r)]$.

(19) $(p \lor q) \leftrightarrow (q \lor p)$.

(The *commutativity* of "$\lor$".)

(20) $(p \land q) \leftrightarrow (q \land p)$.

(The *commutativity* of "$\land$".)

(21) $[(p \lor q) \lor r] \leftrightarrow [p \lor (q \lor r)]$.

(22) $[(p \land q) \land r] \leftrightarrow [p \land (q \land r)]$.

(The *associativity* of "$\lor$" and "$\land$" respectively. On the strength of these laws we will also write

$p \lor q \lor r$ for $(p \lor q) \lor r$ and $p \lor (q \lor r)$,

$p \land q \land r$ for $(p \land q) \land r$ and $p \land (q \land r)$,

because the position of the parentheses has no effect on the truth value.)

(23) $[(p \lor q) \land r] \leftrightarrow [(p \land r) \lor (q \land r)]$.

(24) $[(p \land q) \lor r] \leftrightarrow [(p \lor r) \land (q \lor r)]$.

(The *distributive* laws.)

(25) $[\neg(p \lor q)] \leftrightarrow (\neg p \land \neg q)$.

(26) $[\neg(p \land q)] \leftrightarrow (\neg p \lor \neg q)$.

(The *reciprocity* laws.)

The laws from (19) onward are rather like the similarly named laws for operations on sets. The relation will be shown later on.

(27) $[(p \to r) \land (q \to r)] \leftrightarrow [(p \lor q) \to r]$.

(28) $[(p \to q) \land (p \to r)] \leftrightarrow [p \to (q \land r)]$.

(These two laws can be proved directly or be derived from the distributive laws by means of (15).)

(29) $\neg(p \to q) \leftrightarrow (p \wedge \neg q)$.

(This follows from (15) and (25).)

(30) $[(p \to q) \wedge (r \to s)] \to [(p \wedge r) \to (q \wedge s)]$,
(31) $[(p \to q) \vee (r \to s)] \to [(p \wedge r) \to (q \vee s)]$.

(Proved in 2.6.)

2.11 | *All Propositional Functions*

The table given in 2.3 also contains the connective "$/$".
This by no means exhausts the range of possible connectives, however. We have met connectives that make a new proposition from one or from two given propositions. In more general terms we may wish to know all the operations that make a new proposition from n given propositions

$p_1, \ldots, p_n$.

In other words: we regard $p_1, \ldots, p_n$ as variables which can only have the values 0 (false) and 1 (true), and we seek all the functions F thereof, for which the values

$F(p_1, \ldots, p_n)$

can also be only 0 and 1. How many such functions are there?
First, we inquire as to the *number* of evaluations of the system $p_1, \ldots, p_n$. Such an evaluation is fully determined if we know which of the p_i have the value 1. Hence there are as many of these as there are subsets of a set of n elements, i.e., 2^n (see 1.4). F is completely determined if we know for which evaluation of $p_1, \ldots, p_n$ the $F(p_1, \ldots, p_n)$ will have the value 1. There are therefore as many functions F as there are subsets of a set of 2^n elements, i.e.,

2^{2^n} functions F

of $p_1, \ldots, p_n$. Equivalent F (i.e., with correspondingly equal values) are in this case not regarded as being different.
A function F of one variable p is completely known if we know the table

p	$F(p)$
0	a_1
1	a_2

This function is denoted by $C_{a_1 a_2}$.

C_{00}, which is always 0, can be obtained in the form: $p \land \neg p$ (because this is never true).

C_{11}, which is always 1, can be obtained in the form: $p \lor \neg p$ (which is always true).

$C_{01}(p)$: p.

$C_{10}(p)$: $\neg p$.

A function F of p_1, p_2 is completely known if we know the table

p_1	p_2	$F(p_1, p_2)$
0	0	a_1
0	1	a_2
1	0	a_3
1	1	a_4

This function is designated by $C_{a_1 a_2 a_3 a_4}$.

There are sixteen of them, among which

1, 4, 6, 4, 1, which assume the value 1

0, 1, 2, 3, 4

times. The first and last are dependent neither on p_1 nor on p_2. Of the middle ones there are two which are dependent on p_1 only and two which are dependent on p_2 only (namely, C_{0011} and C_{1100}, which are equivalent to p_1 and $\neg p_1$, and C_{0101} and C_{1010}, which are equivalent to p_2 and $\neg p_2$, respectively).

Furthermore, the value 1 is twice assumed by

$p_1 \leftrightarrow p_2$ and $p_1 \leftrightarrow \neg p_2$.

Finally, there are

$p_1 \land p_2$, $\neg p_1 \land p_2$, $p_1 \land \neg p_2$, $\neg p_1 \land p_2$,

which assume the value 1 only once, and

$p_1 \lor p_2$, $\neg p_1 \lor p_2$, $p_1 \lor \neg p_2$, $\neg p_1 \lor p_2$,

which assume the value 1 three times.

Now consider

$F(p_1, \ldots, p_n)$.

We put

$$F(p_1, \ldots, p_{n-1}, 0) = G(p_1, \ldots, p_{n-1}),$$
$$F(p_1, \ldots, p_{n-1}, 1) = H(p_1, \ldots, p_{n-1}).$$

Then

$$F(p_1, \ldots, p_n) \leftrightarrow ([\neg p_n \rightarrow G(p_1, \ldots, p_{n-1})] \wedge [p_n \rightarrow H(p_1, \ldots, p_{n-1})]).$$

Hence F can be expressed in functions of less than n variables with the aid of the connectives C_{10}, C_{0111}, C_{0001} (or $\neg$, $\vee$, $\wedge$). By successively repeating this reduction process, we find:
Each $F(p_1, \ldots, p_n)$ can (except for equivalence) be represented with the aid of the connectives $\neg$, $\vee$, $\wedge$.
Thanks to

$$(p \wedge q) \leftrightarrow \neg(\neg p \vee \neg q),$$
$$(p \vee q) \leftrightarrow \neg(\neg p \wedge \neg q)$$

we can dispense with one of the connectives, $\vee$ or $\wedge$.
Because of

$$(p \vee q) \leftrightarrow (\neg p \rightarrow q),$$

it is also possible to manage with $\neg$ and $\rightarrow$ only.
The required number of connectives can even be reduced to one, namely, for example the "bar" which occurs in the table in 2.3.
For

$$(p / q) \leftrightarrow (\neg p \wedge \neg q),$$

hence

$$\neg p \leftrightarrow (p / p);$$

furthermore

$$p \wedge q \leftrightarrow ((\neg p) / (\neg q))$$
$$\leftrightarrow ((p / p) / (q / q)).$$

All connectives can be produced with $\neg p \vee \neg q$ also. It can readily be shown that there exist no other functions of two variables which are able to do this.

The Binary System

2.12 | We normally write our numbers using the decimal system with the symbols $0, 1, 2, \ldots, 9$. The position farthest to the right represents the units; the positions to the left of this successively represent the tens, the hundreds, etc. Thus, the nth position represents the 10^{n-1}-folds. Hence

$$a_n a_{n-1} \ldots a_1 a_0 \quad \text{means} \quad a_n \cdot 10^n + a_{n-1} \cdot 10^{n-1} + \ldots + a_1 \cdot 10 + a_0.$$

Electronic computers usually employ the binary system, the only figure symbols being 0 and 1. Each position has twice the value of that of its right-hand neighbour.

$$a_n a_{n-1} \ldots a_1 a_0 \quad \text{means} \quad a_n \cdot 2^n + a_{n-1} \cdot 2^{n-1} + \ldots + a_1 \cdot 2 + a_0.$$

In the binary system the calculations $37 + 30 = 67$, $67 - 30 = 37$, $13 \times 5 = 65$, $65 : 5 = 13$ appear as follows:

```
    100101            1000011           1101      101 / 1000001 \ 1101
  +  11110          -  11110          ×  101          101
    -------           -------           ----          ---
    1000011           100101            1101           110
                                       11010           101
                                       -------          ---
                                       1000001          101
                                                        101
                                                        ---
```

The arithmetical operations are similar to those in the decimal system; only the addition and multiplication are much simpler:

a	b	ab	$a+b$
0	0	0	00
0	1	0	01
1	0	0	01
1	1	1	10

This is reminiscent of the tables used in the logic of propositions:

ab corresponds to $a \wedge b$;
the left-hand figure of $a + b$ corresponds to $a \wedge b$,
and the right-hand figure corresponds to $\neg(a \leftrightarrow b)$ (a and b contradict each other).

2.13 | Variables which can assume exactly two values can be interpreted as propositional variables. For example:

Switch: on or off.
Light: on or off.
Electric conductor: live or dead.
Door: open or closed.

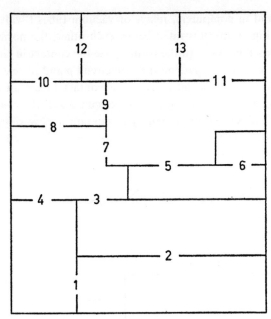

Fig. 4

These values can be conceived as corresponding to "true" or "false" (1 or 0). Fig. 4 represents the plan of the interior of a house. The various numbers correspond to doors. The "ith door open or closed" is taken as corresponding to "p_i true or false". Then the possibility of going from bottom left to top right in the plan is expressed by:

$$[(p_1 \wedge p_2 \wedge p_3) \vee p_4]$$
$$\wedge (\{[p_7 \vee (p_8 \wedge p_9)] \wedge p_{11}\} \vee \{[(p_7 \wedge p_9) \vee p_8] \wedge p_{10} \wedge p_{12} \wedge p_{13}\}).$$

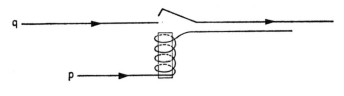

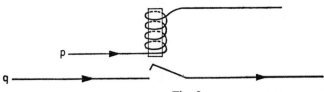

Fig. 5

In telephone exchanges and in computers, relays or vacuum tubes ("valves") are used as switches. In Fig. 5 are illustrated below each other, the normally open and the normally closed contact. In the former case the contact in circuit q is closed if, and only if, a current is passing through circuit p and the electromagnet is therefore activated. In the latter case the contact in circuit q is closed if, and only if, no current is passing through circuit p and the electromagnet is therefore dead. If we assume circuit q to contain a power supply (such as a battery), then the effect of the switch upon the circuit q can be represented by p and $\neg p$ respectively.

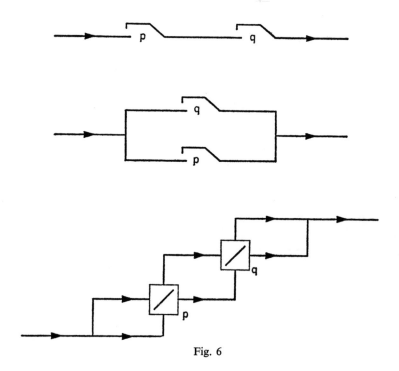

Fig. 6

Fig. 6 gives circuit diagrams for $r =$

       $p \wedge q$ (normally open contacts connected in series),
       $p \vee q$ (normally open contacts parallel connected),
    $\neg(p \leftrightarrow q)$ (two-way switch).

In computers complicated functions of a large number of proposition variables have to be established. It has already been shown how they can all be built up from two types (or even from only one type). It is, of course, essential to do this in the simplest possible way.

The human brain contains billions of elements (neurons) which are susceptible to two states (*viz.*, "activated" and "not activated") and are connected in a vast variety of ways. All sixteen proposition functions of two variables seem to occur there. In the study of brain functions, investigators make use off analogies with the functioning of computers.

3 | SUBJECT AND PREDICATE

"All" and "There is"

3.1 | In Chapter 2 we dealt with the composing of propositions from simpler ones or the breaking up of propositions into less complex ones.

The simplest (atomic) propositions were not further analysed. Grammatical analysis of sentences divides these in parts among which the subject and predicate. In logic these terms are used to denote corresponding notions in the analysis of propositions.

Mathematical propositions may contain variables.

$$(a + b)(a - b) = a^2 - b^2$$

is true for all numbers a, b;

$$x^2 - 3x + 2 = 0$$

is true only for certain x, namely, for $x = 1$ and $x = 2$;

$$(2x + y = 3) \wedge (4x + 2y = 5)$$

is never true (the equations are incompatible).

Other examples (in which the variables run over the set of all people):

    p_1: x lives in London.
    p_2: x lives in England.
    p_3: x is the Lord Mayor of London.
    p_4: x is the father of y.
    p_5: y is the son of x.
    p_6: x is younger than y.
    p_7: y is older than x.
    p_8: y is younger than z.
    p_9: x is younger than z.

All these are propositions which are sometimes true and sometimes false, e.g. p_3 is correct for only *one* x; p_1 is correct for approx. 8,000,000 x; p_2 is correct for approx. 50,000,000 x.

On the other hand, the following propositions are always true:

$$p_3 \rightarrow p_1, \quad p_1 \rightarrow p_2, \quad p_3 \rightarrow p_2,$$
$$[(p_3 \rightarrow p_1) \wedge (p_1 \rightarrow p_2)] \rightarrow (p_3 \rightarrow p_2),$$
$$p_4 \leftrightarrow p_5, \quad p_6 \leftrightarrow p_7, \quad p_6 \rightarrow (p_8 \rightarrow p_9).$$

The propositions

$$p_4 \wedge p_6, \quad p_5 \wedge p_6$$

are never true.

(The example in the second line is still a true proposition, if we replace p_1, p_2, p_3 by any other proposition. In the other lines, we have to insert for p_1, p_2, p_3, the propositions indicated above.)

As soon as we have to deal with propositions in which a variable occurs, we need symbols that express whether a proposition is always, sometimes or never true.

3.2 | A proposition like $F(x)$, in which there is a variable x, represents a whole system of propositions in the sense of chapter 2; we obtain this system, by substituting for the variable x the individuals a, b, c,..., over which x is running:

$$F(a), F(b), F(c), \ldots .$$

For example, we may substitute for x in $p_1(x)$ after each other all people; we obtain then propositions like in 2 such as:

The worldchampion jiu-jitsu lives in London,
Brigitte Bardot lives in London,
The Lord Mayor of London lives in London,

some of which are true and some are not.

With a constant proposition p, like we know them from 2, we had two possibilities: it was true or false. We could even satisfy ourselves with only one truth-value (e.g. "true"); the falseness of p being expressed by the truth of $\neg p$. Do we need now a differentiated concept of truth for these variable-dependent propositions, or can we insert this "always", "sometimes", "never" with the word "true" into the proposition, just like we replaced "p false" by "$\neg p$ true"?

If a proposition $F(x)$ like

$$x \text{ lives in London} \rightarrow x \text{ lives in England}$$

is to be always true, then this means that,

$$F(a), F(b), F(c), \ldots$$

are true, or in other words that the conjunction

$$F(a) \wedge F(b) \wedge F(c) \wedge \ldots$$

is true. This is a cumbersome formula, especially if the variables x in $F(x)$ are allowed to run over infinitely many individuals. Instead of this we therefore write

$$\bigwedge_x F(x),$$

and we read this as

for all x, $F(x)$.

$F(x)$ always true, i.e. true for all x, is now expressed by

$\bigwedge_x F(x)$ is true.

Herewith we have inserted the "always"-differentiation with "true" into the proposition, of which the truth is asserted. Similarly we do this with "sometimes". If a proposition $F(x)$ like

x lives in London

is to be true sometimes, then this means that at least one of the propositions

$F(a), F(b), F(c), \ldots$

has to be true, or in other words, the disjunction

$F(a) \lor F(b) \lor F(c) \lor \ldots$

is true. Here too we simplify this notation to

$$\bigvee_x F(x),$$

which we read as

there is an x, so that $F(x)$.

$F(x)$ true for some x, is now expressed by

$\bigvee_x F(x)$ is true.

Herewith we have inserted the "sometimes"-differentiation with "true" into the proposition, the truth of which is being asserted. (Note: "there is an $x, \ldots$" does not mean, that there is only one such x; there may be more. This may even be all. "All" is a special case of "some".) $F(x)$ never true, is clearly the same as, there is no x for which $F(x)$ is true, i.e. $\bigvee_x F(x)$ is not true, or formulated in still another way

$$\neg \bigvee_x F(x)$$

is true.

3.3 | $\wedge$ and $\vee$ are called *quantifiers,* because they indicate for how many (quantum) values of the variable the proposition is true. In

$$\wedge_x F(x) \quad \text{and} \quad \vee_x F(x)$$

x no longer occurs as a variable but is *bound.*
There are also other ways to *bind* variables. We know already the method of doing this by *substitution* of an individual for the variable, e.g., substitution of "Mars" or "Sirius" for x in

x is a planet

(in the former case it is true, in the latter false).
Note that

$$(\wedge_x F(x)) \rightarrow F(a),$$
$$F(a) \rightarrow \vee_x F(x)$$

are true.

3.4 | In a proposition different variables may be bound in different ways. Take

x is mother of y,

abbreviated xMy.
Then for

$$\vee_y (xMy)$$

we may also read: x is a mother.
One variable has been eliminated by binding; the other is still free. We can also bind this x:

$$\vee_x \vee_y (xMy)$$

means: there is a mother.

$$\wedge_x \vee_y (xMy)$$

means: everyone is a mother.
Of course, this is false. But the following is true:

$$\neg \wedge_x \vee_y (xMy).$$

We can, however, also start with the x:

$$\vee_x (xMy)$$

means: y is a child.*)

*) Always supplement this by "of a mother".

$$\bigvee_y \bigvee_x (xMy)$$

means: there is a child.

$$\bigwedge_y \bigvee_x (xMy) \tag{*}$$

means: everyone is a child.
This is true.
We can also start with the universal quantifier:

$$\bigwedge_y (xMy)$$

means: x is everyone's mother.

$$\bigwedge_x \bigwedge_y (xMy)$$

means: everyone is everyone's mother.

$$\bigvee_x \bigwedge_y (xMy) \tag{**}$$

means: there is a mother of all.
Or, again starting with x:

$$\bigwedge_x (xMy)$$

means: y is everyone's child.

$$\bigwedge_y \bigwedge_x (xMy)$$

means: everyone is everyone's child.

$$\bigvee_y \bigwedge_x (xMy)$$

means: there is some one who is everyone's child.
Note more particular that (*) and (**), which differ only in the order in which the quantifiers occur, have different truth values.

3.5 | On the other hand, in the case of similar quantifiers the order in which in which they occur does not matter:

$\bigvee_x \bigvee_y (xMy)$ (there is a mother),
$\bigvee_y \bigvee_x (xMy)$ (there is a child),
$\bigvee_{x,y} (xMy)$ (there is a pair "mother-child")

are equivalent. Generalizing, it is true that

$$\bigvee_x \bigvee_y F(x, y), \quad \bigvee_y \bigvee_x F(x, y), \quad \bigvee_{x,y} F(x, y)$$

are equivalent.

(The notation $\ulcorner x, y \urcorner$ had been agreed upon for the directed pair of x and y, but this has here been simplified for typographical reasons.)

How can we verify the equivalence of the above propositions? For the variables we substitute all possible individuals $a, b, c, \ldots$ and write down

$F(a, a),$	$F(a, b),$	$F(a, c),$	$\cdots$	$\bigvee_y F(a, y)$
$F(b, a),$	$F(b, b),$	$F(b, c),$	$\cdots$	$\bigvee_y F(b, y)$
$F(c, a),$	$F(c, b),$	$F(c, c),$	$\cdots$	$\bigvee_y F(c, y)$
$\vdots$	$\vdots$	$\vdots$		$\vdots$
$\bigvee_x F(x, a),$	$\bigvee_x F(x, b),$	$\bigvee_x F(x, c),$	$\cdots$	

After the ith row is written the disjunction of what is stated in the ith row; and under the jth column is written the disjunction of what is stated in the jth column. The disjunction of the last column is

$$\bigvee_x \bigvee_y F(x, y).$$

In order to verify the truth of this, we must find something that is true in the last column, and in order to verify the truth of something in the last column, we must find something that is true in the row thereof. It therefore all boils down to finding a pair $\ulcorner x, y \urcorner$ for which $F(x, y)$ is true, i.e.,

$$\bigvee_{x,y} F(x, y).$$

The same applies to

$$\bigvee_y \bigvee_x F(x, y).$$

In this case we have to run over the scheme in the opposite way, hence first the columns and then the rows.

3.6 | We can similarly show that

$$\bigwedge_x \bigwedge_y F(x, y), \quad \bigwedge_y \bigwedge_x F(x, y), \quad \bigwedge_{x,y} F(x, y)$$

are equivalent.

An analogous proof can be given for more than two variables.

3.7 | If p is independent of x, then of course

$$\bigvee_x p \leftrightarrow p$$

and $\bigwedge_x p \leftrightarrow p$

are true.

3.8 | The distributive laws (23), (24) (see 2.10) lead to similar laws for $\vee$ and $\wedge$. Let p be independent of x. Then

$$[p \wedge \vee_x F(x)] \leftrightarrow [\vee_x(p \wedge F(x))],$$
$$[p \vee \wedge_x F(x)] \leftrightarrow [\wedge_x(p \vee F(x))].$$

To prove this, write down:

$$[p \wedge (F(a) \vee F(b) \vee F(c) \vee \ldots)] \leftrightarrow (p \wedge F(a)) \vee (p \wedge F(b)) \vee$$
$$\vee (p \wedge F(c)) \vee \ldots)$$

etc.

3.9 | There exists a similar analogy with (27) and (28) in 2.10; true are

$$[\wedge_x(F(x) \to p)] \leftrightarrow [(\vee_x F(x)) \to p],$$
$$[\wedge_x(p \to F(x))] \leftrightarrow [p \to \wedge_x F(x)].$$

3.10 | What is the negation of

"all men are mortal"?

Not

"all men are immortal",

for the first statement is refuted even if only one immortal human being can be found. The true negation of the above statement is therefore

"there is a man who is not mortal".

In general we seek an equivalent of

$$\neg\wedge_x F(x).$$

If for this we write again

$$\neg(F(a) \wedge F(b) \wedge F(c) \wedge \ldots)$$

and apply (26) (see 2.10), we find

$$\neg F(a) \vee \neg F(b) \vee \neg F(c) \vee \ldots,$$

hence

$$\vee_x \neg F(x).$$

The negation of "$F(x)$ holds for all x" is therefore "there is an x for which not-$F(x)$ holds"; hence

$$(\neg\wedge_x F(x)) \leftrightarrow (\vee_x \neg F(x)).$$

If we take more particularly for $F(x)$

$(x$ is a man$) \rightarrow (x$ is mortal$)$,

we then obtain the true proposition

$$\{\neg \wedge_x[(x \text{ is a man}) \rightarrow (x \text{ is mortal})]\}$$
$$\leftrightarrow \{\vee_x\neg[(x \text{ is a man}) \rightarrow (x \text{ is mortal})]\},$$

or applying (29) (see 2.10)

$$\leftrightarrow \{\vee_x[(x \text{ is a man}) \wedge \neg(x \text{ is mortal})]\}.$$

3.11 | Similarly is true

$$(\neg\vee_x F(x)) \leftrightarrow (\wedge_x\neg F(x)).$$

The statement on the left is: there is no x for which $F(x)$ holds.
On the right: for all x, not-$F(x)$ holds.
The laws in 3.10–11 can be summarized in the following words:
We may interchange $\neg$ and a quantifier if the latter is reversed at the same time.
This recalls the reciprocity laws stated in 2.10 (25–26) and similar laws applicable to operations on sets.

3.12 | *Problems*

The following notation will be employed:
$M(x)$: x is male,
$V(x)$: x is female,
xJy: x is younger than y,
xKy: x is a child of y,
xGy: x is married to y,
$U(x)$: x lives at Utrecht,
$A(x)$: x lives at Amsterdam.
where all the variables relate to people.
Now write down the symbolic expressions for:
1. Everyone has a father and a mother.
2. Whoever has a father, also has a mother.
3. Everyone is younger than his or her parents.
4. Everyone is younger than his or her grandparents.
5. x is married.
6. There is a man with a daughter-in-law who is older than he is.

7. x and y are brothers (i.e., full brothers).

8.   If there is woman at Utrecht with a brother at Amsterdam then there is a man at Amsterdam with a sister at Utrecht.

9.   A married man need not live at Utrecht.

10.   Not every woman at Utrecht has no son at Amsterdam.

11.   All the children of x are married.

12.   There is some one, all of whose children are married.

13.   Every child of x is married to a child of y.

14.   There is a child of y who is not married to a child of x.

15.   There are two people, each child of one of them is married to a child of the other.

16.   There are two people, no child of one of them is married to a child of the other.

17.   If y is a child of x, then every child of y is a grandchild of x.

And further:

18.   Read $\bigwedge_y \{[\bigwedge_x (xKy \to U(y))] \leftrightarrow [(\bigvee_x xKy) \to U(y)]\}$
and find out what this has to do with 3.9.

Read the following formulae and find out on the basis of which laws they are true (independently of the meaning of K, G, U, etc.).

19. $\neg \bigwedge_x \{[\bigvee_y (xGy)] \to U(x)\} \leftrightarrow \bigvee_x (\bigvee_y (xGy) \wedge \neg U(x))$.

20. $[\neg \bigwedge_y \bigvee_x (xKy)] \leftrightarrow [\bigvee_y \bigwedge_x \neg (xKy)]$.

21. $\bigvee_x \bigwedge_y (yKx \to \bigvee_z (zKy)) \leftrightarrow \neg \bigwedge_x \bigvee_y [yKx \wedge \bigwedge_z (\neg (zKy))]$.

The following notation will now be introduced:

$Z(x, t)$: I see the thing x at the instant t.

$P(x, t)$: I seize the thing x at the instant t.

$t' < t$: the instant t' precedes the instant t.

Write the symbolic expressions for:

22.   I always see something.

23.   Sometimes I see nothing.

24.   There are things that I never see.

25.   I see each thing once at some time.

26.   If I see something, I seize it immediately.

27.   If I see something, I seize it some time later.

28.   Before I seize something, I have seen it.

29.   If I seize something without having seen it, then I see it some time later without seizing it.

30.   There is nothing that I do not seize at some time.

31. What I always see I never seize.
32. At every instant there are things that I neither see nor seize.
33. I seize everything that I do not see all the time.
34. I seize everything unless I have already seized it before.
35. I always see everything or nothing.
36. If I seize something that I have seen before, then I have earlier seen something that I seized later on.
37. Some things that I have seen earlier, I always see again at some later time.
38. If I have ever seen two things simultaneously, then in the future I shall also see them only simultaneously.
39. If I have ever simultaneously seen and seized a thing, then later I do this successively or not at all.

Next the variables will be assumed to run over the real numbers, while the algebraic signs have their usual meaning.
Read and find out whether the following propositions are true:

40. $\wedge_{x,y}(x+y=y+x)$.
41. $\wedge_x\vee_y(x+y=3)$.
42. $\vee_y\wedge_x(x+y=3)$.
43. $\vee_x\vee_y(x+y=3)$.
44. $\wedge_{x,y}(x+y=3)$.
45. $(\wedge_{x,y}(x+y=3)) \rightarrow (2=3)$.
46. $\vee_{x,y}[(x>y>0) \wedge (x+y=0)]$.
47. $\wedge_a\{[\vee_x(ax=6)] \leftrightarrow (a\neq 0)\}$.
48. $\wedge_x\{(x^2>x) \leftrightarrow [(x>1) \vee (x<0)]\}$.
49. $\wedge_{a,b,c}\{[\vee_x(ax^2+bx+c=0)] \leftrightarrow (b^2-4ac\geq 0)\}$.
50. $\wedge_{a,b,c}\{[\wedge_x(ax^2+bx+c>0)] \leftrightarrow [(b^2-4ac<0) \wedge (a>0)]\}$.
51. $\wedge_x\{[(x>2) \wedge \neg(x>3)] \leftrightarrow (2<x\leq 3)\}$.
52. $\wedge_x\{[(x>2) \wedge (x<1)] \leftrightarrow (x\neq x)\}$.
53. $\wedge_x\{[(x>1) \vee (x<2)] \leftrightarrow (x=x)\}$.
54. $\wedge_{a,b}[\{\vee_x[(x>a) \wedge (x<b)]\} \leftrightarrow (a<b)]$.
55. $\wedge_{a,b}([\wedge_x\{(x^2+ax+b=0) \rightarrow [(x=1) \vee (x=2)]\}]$
    $\rightarrow [(a=-3) \wedge (b=2)])$.
56. $\wedge_b\{[\vee_a\wedge_x(x^2+ax+b>0)] \leftrightarrow (b>0)\}$.
57. $\wedge_b\vee_a\wedge_x(x^2+ax+b>0)$.
58. $\wedge_b\{[\wedge_a\vee_x(x^2+ax+b=0)] \leftrightarrow (b\leq 0)\}$.
59. $\vee_b\wedge_a\vee_x(x^2+ax+b=0)$.
60. $\vee_a\wedge_b\vee_x(x^2+ax+b=0)$.

3.13 | One of the above problems should by rights have been accompanied by a warning.

"If from $x^2 + ax + b = 0$ follows $x = 1$ or $x = 2$, then $a = -3$ and $b = 2$ (a, x, b are assumed to run over all real numbers)."

Is this true?

No!

Because, for example, "$x^2 + 1 = 0$" also implies "$x = 1$ or $x = 2$" (for any x) — since $x^2 + 1 = 0$ is false (for any x) and we know that $p \to q$ is true when p is false. Hence

$$\bigwedge_x \{(x^2 + ax + b = 0) \to [(x = 1) \lor (x = 2)]\} \tag{*}$$

is, for example, also true if $a = 0$, $b = 1$. We, therefore, may not infer from (*) that $(a = -3) \land (b = 2)$ holds, as was asserted in 3.12.55.

Instead of $x^2 + 1 = 0$ we could have chosen, as another counter example, any other quadratic equation that has no (real) solution. Even for example $x^2 - 2x + 1 = 0$ or $x^2 - 4x + 4 = 0$, for

$$\bigwedge_x [(x^2 - 2x + 1 = 0) \to (x = 1)],$$

hence certainly

$$\bigwedge_x [(x^2 - 2x + 1) = 0) \to (x = 1 \lor x = 2)],$$

and analogously with the other example. We may truly assert:

$$\bigwedge_{a,b} (\bigwedge_x \{(x^2 + ax + b = 0) \to [(x = 1) \lor (x = 2)]\}$$
$$\to \{[(a = -3) \land (b = 2)] \lor \neg\bigvee_{x,y}[(x \neq y) \land (x^2 + ax + b = y^2 + ay + b = 0)]\}),$$

or

$$\bigwedge_{a,b} (\bigvee_{x,y}[(x \neq y) \land (x^2 + ax + b = y^2 + ay + b = 0)]$$
$$\to (\bigwedge_x \{(x^2 + ax + b = 0) \to [(x = 1) \to (x = 2)]\}) \to [(a = -3) \land$$
$$\land (b = 2)]).$$

For those who still refuse to believe that for all x

$$(x^2 + 1 = 0) \to [(x = 1) \lor (x = 2)]$$

is true:

Let $x^2 + 1 = 0$. Then

$$0 \leq x^2 = -1 \leq 0,$$
hence $\quad 0 = x^2 = -1 = 0$.

Therefore $x = 0$,
and since $0 = -1$, also
$$0 = 1,$$
hence $x = 1$, so that
certainly $(x = 1) \lor (x = 2)$.

The Set of All ...

3.14 | The x, for which

     x is a human being

is true, form a set, namely, the set of human beings. The x, for which

     $x^2 - 3x - 2 = 0$

is true, form a set comprising the numbers 1 and 2.
Let $F(x)$ again be a proposition dependent upon x.
Then the x, for which $F(x)$ is true, form a set which we shall designate as

     $\uparrow_x F(x)$.

Hence

     $\uparrow_x(x$ is a human being$)$ = set of human beings,
     $\uparrow_x(x^2 - 3x + 2 = 0) = (1, 2)$.

In general we shall say that

     $\bigwedge_z [(z \in \uparrow_x F(x)) \leftrightarrow F(z)]$.

Any z belongs to $\uparrow_x F(x)$ if, and only if, $F(z)$ is true.
Let x run over a certain "total" T (e.g., all human beings or all real numbers).
If $F(x)$ is always true, then $\uparrow_x F(x)$ equals T.
If $F(x)$ is never true, then $\uparrow_x F(x)$ is the empty set.
$\uparrow_x F(x)$ and $\uparrow_x \neg F(x)$ are each other's complements.

$[\bigwedge_x(F(x) \rightarrow G(x))] \leftrightarrow [(\uparrow_x F(x)) \subset (\uparrow_x G(x))]$.

Proof: Suppose

     $\bigwedge_x(F(x) \rightarrow G(x))$ (1)

to be true.
Now let

     $a \in (\uparrow_x F(x))$.   (2)

We must show that also $a \in (\uparrow_x G(x))$. From (1) follows in particular that

$$F(a) \to G(a);$$

from (2) follows, having regard to the definition of $\uparrow$:

$$F(a).$$

Hence (modus ponens)

$$G(a).$$

Hence (definition of $\uparrow$)

$$a \in (\uparrow_x G(x)).$$

Herewith one half of the statement has been proved. The reader is invited to prove the other half for himself.

$$\uparrow_x(F(x) \wedge G(x)) = (\uparrow_x F(x)) \cap (\uparrow_x G(x)).$$
$$\uparrow_x(F(x) \vee G(x)) = (\uparrow_x F(x)) \cup (\uparrow_x G(x)).$$

He is likewise invited to prove these formulae!

In 2.10 we had our attention called to the similarity in laws (19)–(24) for, $\cup$, $\cap$, on one hand, and, on the other hand, $\vee$, $\wedge$. This is not an accidental similarity, as appears from the last two formulae. The similarity also extends to $\neg$ and * (complement-forming) respectively (2.10.25–26). Where did we just encounter the relationship between $\neg$ and *?

3.15 | Problems

Using the notation indicated in 3.12, write down:
1. The set of the inhabitants of Amsterdam.
2. The set of the married inhabitants of Amsterdam.
3. The set of the children of y.
4. The set of all married couples.
5. The set of all instants at which I see things without seizing them.
6. The set of all things that I seize without first having seen them.
7. Check whether $\uparrow_{x,y} \ulcorner xKy, \uparrow_x \uparrow_y xKy, \uparrow_y \uparrow_x xKy$ are the same.

Check whether (for real numbers) the following propositions are true:

8. $[\uparrow \ulcorner_{a,b,c} \urcorner \vee_x (ax^2 + bx + c = 0)] = \{]\uparrow \ulcorner_{a,b,c} \urcorner (b^2 - 4ac \geq 0)]$
$$\cap \uparrow \ulcorner_{a,b,c} \urcorner [(a = b = 0) \to (c = 0)]\}.$$
9. $\uparrow_x(x^2 + 1 = 0) = \uparrow_x(x^2 + 2 = 0)$.

10. $\uparrow_a \wedge_y (\{a \in [\uparrow_x (xy = 0)]\} \to (y = 0)) = \uparrow_a \vee_b (ab = 1)$.

11. $\uparrow_x [(x - 1)(x - 2)(x - 3)(x - 4) > 0]$
$= \{[\uparrow_x (x < 1)] \cup [\uparrow_x (2 < x < 3)] \cup [\uparrow_x (x > 4)]\}$.

12. $\wedge_{a,b,c,d} (\{\uparrow_x [(x^2 + ax + b)(x^2 + cx + d) = 0]\}$
$= \{[\uparrow_x (x^2 + ax + b = 0)] \cup [\uparrow_x (x^2 + cx + d = 0)]\})$.

13. $\uparrow_b \vee_a \wedge_x (x^2 + ax + b > 0) = \uparrow_b \vee_a (a^2 < b)$.

Let A be a set.

14.   What is $\uparrow_X (X \subset A)$?

Let B be another set. Check whether is true:

15. $\uparrow_X (X \subset A) \cap \uparrow_X (X \subset B) = \uparrow_X (X \subset A \cap B)$.

16. $\uparrow_X (X \subset A) \cup \uparrow_X (X \subset B) = \uparrow_X (X \subset A \cup B)$.

17. $\uparrow_X (X \subset A) \setminus \uparrow_X (X \subset B) = \uparrow_X (X \subset A \setminus B)$.

Let the small letters only run over the set of natural numbers and let x Div y denote the proposition "x is a divisor of y", i.e.,

$$\wedge_{x,y} [x \text{ Div } y \leftrightarrow \vee_z (xz = y)].$$

18.   What is $\uparrow_x x$ Div y?

19.   What is $\uparrow_y x$ Div y?

20.   What is $\uparrow_x x$ Div $y \cap \uparrow_x x$ Div z?

21.   What is $\uparrow_z x$ Div $z \cap \uparrow_z y$ Div z?

In answering the last three questions use the terms "multiple of ...", "common divisor of ...", "common multiple of ...".

22.   What is $\uparrow_x x$ Div $a \cap \uparrow_x a$ Div x?

23.   What is $\uparrow_x ((x \text{ Div } a) \wedge \wedge_y \{(y \text{ Div } x) \to [(y = 1) \vee (y = x)]\})$?

In 1.22 we divided a set Ω into equivalence classes. Let an equivalence relation be given in the set Ω; the elements of Ω are designated by small letters; "$x \sim y$" means "x equivalent to y".

24.   What is the meaning of $\uparrow_x (x \sim y)$?

25.   Is $\wedge_{y,z} ([z \in \uparrow_x (x \sim y] \to [\uparrow_x (x \sim y) = \uparrow_x (x \sim z)])$ true?

26.   Verify that

$$\uparrow_A \{\vee_y [A = \uparrow_x (x \sim y)]\}$$

means: the set of all equivalence classes (in Ω).

27.   Verify (see 1.25):

$$\ulcorner A, B\urcorner = \uparrow z \vee x,y[(x \in A) \wedge (y \in B) \wedge (z = \ulcorner x, y^1\urcorner)].$$

3.16 | In the first chapter we considered unions and intersections of finite numbers of sets only. We did, however, encounter several instances of "sets of sets".

Let N be the set of natural numbers and R be the set of real numbers.

Let M_n be the set of the numbers $\leqq \dfrac{1}{n}$, hence

$$M_n = \uparrow x[(x \in R) \wedge (x \leqq \frac{1}{n})].$$

The intersection of all M_n is the set

$$\uparrow x[(x \in R) \wedge (x \leqq 0)].$$

This intersection is also denoted by

$$\bigcap_{n \in N} M_n.$$

Let P_a be the set of the real numbers $\leqq a$. We shall consider all sets P_a with $a \in R \backslash P_0$. Their intersection is P_0:

$$\bigcap_{a \in R \backslash P_0} P_a = P_0.$$

In general, suppose we have a system of sets M_n which have been distinguished by a subscript n, n running over an arbitrary set N. Their intersection is denoted by

$$\bigcap_{n \in N} M_n$$

i.e.,

$$c \in \bigcap_{n \in N} M_n \leftrightarrow \wedge n[(n \in N) \rightarrow (c \in M_n)].$$

Note the relationship between $\bigcap$ and $\wedge$.

We can similarly define the union of the sets M_n ($n \in N$) by

$$c \in \bigcup_{n \in N} M_n \leftrightarrow \vee n[(n \in N) \rightarrow (c \in M_n)].$$

This is the relationship between $\bigcup$ and $\vee$.

If there can be no misunderstanding as to the set to which the subscript belongs, the notation may be simplified to $\bigcup_n M_n$ and $\bigcap_n M_n$ respectively.

A relation with 3.14 is:

Let $F(x, y)$ be a proposition dependent upon x and y; here again x can run over a total T, and y runs over a set N which is not related to T. Now for each $n \in N$

we consider the set M_n of all x for which $F(x, n)$ is true, and we take their intersection:

$$\bigcap_n \uparrow_x F(x, n) = \uparrow_x \bigwedge_n F(x, n).$$

Think of the case where N consists only of two elements and compare this with the penultimate formula in 3.14.
Similarly

$$\bigcup_n \uparrow_x F(x, n) = \uparrow_x \bigvee_n F(x, n).$$

Compare this with the last formula in 3.14.

3.17 | Problems

The notation used in 3.15 will be employed.

1.   What is $\bigcap_Y \uparrow_X (X \subset Y \subset A)$?
2.   What is $\bigcup_Y \uparrow_X (X \subset Y \subset A)$?

If small letters denote natural numbers, then:

3.   What is $\bigcap_x \uparrow_y x \text{ Div } y$?
4.   What is $\bigcup_y \uparrow_x x \text{ Div } y$?
5.   What is $\bigcup_n \uparrow_z \bigvee_x \bigwedge_y ((z = x^n) \wedge \{y \text{ Div } x \rightarrow [(y = 1) \vee (y = x)]\})$?
6.   What is $\bigcap_a \uparrow_x \bigvee_y (x = ay + 1)$?

The Article

3.18 | We speak of *the* solution of $3x = 2$, but not of *the* solution of $0x = 3$ or of *the* solution of $x^2 - 5x + 6 = 0$. We speak of *the* x with the property E if there is one and only one x that has the property E. If E is the property, to turn $F(x)$ into a true proposition then the condition for speaking of *the* x is

$$\bigvee_x F(x) \wedge \bigwedge_{x,y} [(F(x) \wedge F(y)) \rightarrow (x = y)].$$

(Note that we must have a relation "$=$" at our disposal to be able to write this down.)
The x with the property $F(x)$ is designated by

$$\downarrow_x F(x).$$

Let us, just for the present, confine ourselves to real numbers. How do we write: the largest x for which $x^2 - x \leq 5$? Answer:

$$\downarrow_x\{(x^2 - x \leq 5) \wedge \wedge_y[(y^2 - y \leq 5) \to (y \leq x)]\}.$$

How do we write: the smallest set of which the numbers 288 and 120 are members and of which, with two numbers a and b, $a - b$ is also a member? Answer: We define a proposition $F(X)$ about sets X by:

$$F(X) \leftrightarrow \{(120 \in X) \wedge (288 \in X) \wedge \wedge_{a,b}([(a \in X) \wedge (b \in X)] \to$$
$$\to (a - b \in X))\}.$$

Are there sets X that satisfy $F(X)$? Of course, the set of all numbers satisfies it. If X is such a set, then $288 \in X$, and $120 \in X$, hence $168 = 288 - 120 \in X$, hence $168 - 120 = 48 \in X$, hence $120 - 48 = 72 \in X$, hence $72 - 48 = 24 \in X$. Furthermore $0 = 24 - 24 \in X$, $-24 = 0 - 24 \in X$. All multiplies 24 m (where m is an integer) of 24 are members of X (why?). Let A denote the set of all these multiples. Then

$$F(A)$$

holds (why?). We now just proved:

$$\wedge_X[F(X) \to (X \supset A)].$$

Hence: $F(A)$ is true, and every X for which $F(X)$ is true will include A. Therefore A is the smallest set X with the property $F(X)$.

We may ask ourselves the following question: in general let M be a set of sets X determined by a proposition $F(X)$ about sets X, i.e.,

$$\wedge_X[(X \in M) \leftrightarrow F(X)].$$

Is there a smallest set A in M, i.e., an A such that

$$(A \in M) \wedge \wedge_X[(X \in M) \to (X \supset A)]$$

is true? In general, something of this kind need not exist. (Counter-example: the set M of all *non-empty* subsets of the set (a, b); M will then consist of (a), (b) and (a, b).)

An A as required must be contained in every $X \in M$; hence also

$$A \subset \bigcap_{X \in M} X.$$

But since A must also occur among the $X \in M$,

$$\bigcap_{X \in M} X \subset A$$

must be true and therefore

$$A = \bigcap_{X \in M} X.$$

Hence it immediately follows that there is at most one such a set.

$$(\bigcap_{X \in M} X) \in M$$

need not always be true (see the counter-example). But if it is true, then

$$\bigcap_{X \in M} X$$

is the smallest set of M, because

$$(\bigcap_{X \in M} X) \subset Y \quad \text{for every} \quad Y \in M.$$

By virtue of this criterion we can again show that there is a smallest set of which 120 and 288 are members and of which, with a and b, $a - b$ is also a member. This is apparent from the following. Let M be the set of all these sets. For every $X \in M$ is $120 \in X$, hence $120 \in \bigcap_{X \in M} X$. Similarly for 288. Furthermore: if $a \in \bigcap_{X \in M} X$ and $b \in \bigcap_{X \in M} X$, then $a \in X$ for all $X \in M$, and $b \in X$ for all $X \in M$; hence $a - b \in X$ for all $X \in M$, and therefore $a - b \in \bigcap_{X \in M} X$. Thus $\bigcap_{X \in M} X$ meets all the requirements on the sets belonging to M. Hence $\bigcap_{X \in M} X$ is the smallest set that is a member of M.

(In this last section the word "all" has repeatedly been used. Rewrite it, using the logic symbols as much as possible.)

Predicates, Relations

3.19 | In this chapter, we often used schemes like

     ... is mortal,
     ... lives at Amsterdam,
     ... is a child of ...,
     ... is equivalent to ...

In each case the dots represent something that must be filled in (humans, elements of a certain set, etc.). We thus obtain propositions which may be false or true.

Expressions of this kind with one free place are called properties or *predicates*; those with two or more free places are known as *relations*. What we fill in at the free places are called *subjects*.

Relations may, however, also be conceived as predicates, namely, predicates of subject-pairs, subject-trios, etc. "... lives at Amsterdam" is a property of individual people; "... is a child of ..." is a property of pairs of persons, in fact, directed pairs. "x is a child of y" is a proposition which may be true for certain pairs x, y and false for others (if it is true for the pair $\ulcorner x, y \urcorner$, it is certainly false for the pair $\ulcorner y, x \urcorner$).

The predicate "... lives at Amsterdam" is fully known to me, if I know the set of all those x which, when filled in, turn the predicate into a true proposition, and *vice versa*. Similarly, the relation "... is a child of ..." is fully known to me if I know the set all those pairs $\ulcorner x, y \urcorner$ which, on being consecutively filled in, turn the relation into a true proposition.

Let $F(\ldots, \ldots)$ be a relation with two free places. Suppose that elements of a set M may be filled in at the first place, and elements of a set N at the second place. (For example $Z(\ldots, \ldots)$ from 3.12; at the first place we may fill in *things*, at the second, *instants*.) Consider the set

$$P = \ulcorner M, N \urcorner,$$

consisting of all $\ulcorner x, y \urcorner$ with $x \in M$, $y \in N$ (see 1.25).

We can now conceive the relation $F(\ldots, \ldots)$ as a predicate $G(\ldots)$ where elements of P may be filled in at the free place and for which holds:

$$\wedge_{x,y}[G(\ulcorner x, y \urcorner) \leftrightarrow F(x, y)].$$

1.24 contains a definition: "A set is said to be ordered by means of a relation "<", if ...". We can now re-define this, without referring to a relation. We replace the relation "... smaller than ..." by the set Y of the pairs which make the relation true when filled in:

A set Z is said to be ordered by means of a set

$$Y \subset \ulcorner Z, Z \urcorner,$$

if

$$\wedge_{a,b}\{[(a \in Z) \wedge (b \in Z) \wedge (a \neq b)] \to [(\ulcorner a, b \urcorner \in Y) \leftrightarrow (\ulcorner b, a \urcorner \notin Y)]\}$$
$$\wedge \ \wedge_{a,b,c}\{[(a \in Z) \wedge (b \in Z) \wedge (c \in Z)$$
$$\wedge \ (\ulcorner a, b \urcorner \in Y) \wedge (\ulcorner b, c \urcorner \in Y)] \to (\ulcorner a, c \urcorner \in Y)\}.$$

3.20 | The definition of a mapping can similarly be re-formulated (see 1.12). A mapping f of A into B is fully known to me if I know all those members $\ulcorner a, b \urcorner$ of $\ulcorner A, B \urcorner$ which have the property that b is the f-image of a. I may even regard f as the set of these pairs $\ulcorner a, b \urcorner$ hence $f \subset \ulcorner A, B \urcorner$. Which parts of $\ulcorner A, B \urcorner$ are then mappings of A into B? We shall designate the set of the mappings of A into B by:

$$A \frown B.$$

Then

$$(f \in A \frown B) \leftrightarrow$$
$$\big[f \subset \ulcorner A, B \urcorner$$
$$\wedge \ \bigwedge_a [(a \in A) \rightarrow (\bigvee_b (\ulcorner a, b \urcorner \in f)]$$
$$\wedge \ \bigwedge_{a,b,c} \{[(\ulcorner a, b \urcorner \in f) \wedge (\ulcorner a, c \urcorner \in f)] \rightarrow (b = c)\}\big].$$

The f-image of a is then

$$fa = \downarrow_b (\ulcorner a, b \urcorner \in f).$$

3.21 | With the aid of the now available symbols we shall give the successive steps in the proof of the theorem stated in 1.19:

(1) $\Omega = \uparrow_X (X \subset A)$.

(2) $A_0 \subset A$.

(3) $f \in (A_0 \frown \Omega)$.

(4) $\bigwedge_X \{(X \in \Omega) \rightarrow [\bigvee_x ((x \in A_0) \wedge (f(x) = X)]\}$.

(5) $U = \uparrow_x [(x \in A_0) \wedge (x \notin f(x))]$.

(6) $\bigwedge_x \{(x \in U) \leftrightarrow [(x \in A_0) \wedge (x \notin f(x))]\}$.

(7) $\bigvee_x [(x \in A_0) \wedge (f(x) = U)]$.

(8) $(u \in A_0) \wedge (f(u) = U)$.

(9) $u \in A_0$.

(10) $f(u) = U$.

(11) $(u \in U) \leftrightarrow [(u \in A_0) \wedge (u \notin f(u))]$.

(12) $(u \in U) \leftrightarrow [(u \in A_0) \wedge (u \notin U)]$.

(13) $(u \in A_0) \rightarrow \{[(u \in A_0) \wedge (u \notin U)] \leftrightarrow u \notin U\}$.

(14) $[(u \in A_0) \wedge (u \notin U)] \leftrightarrow (u \notin U)$.

(15) $(u \in U) \leftrightarrow (u \notin U)$.

(16) $(u \notin U) \leftrightarrow \neg (u \in U)$.

(17) $(u \in U) \leftrightarrow \neg (u \in U)$.

Explanation:

(1)   Definition of Ω as the set of the subsets.

(2)   Assumption of the A_0 and of the

(3) f, which has to map A_0 into Ω and even

(4)   onto Ω.

(5)   Definition of U.

(6) The same with other words.
(7) U has an inverse-image with respect to f, which is denoted by
(8) u.
(9)–(10)   Follow from (8).
(11) By substitution of u for x into (6).
(12) Replacing $f(u)$ by U according to (10).
(13) $q \rightarrow [(q \wedge p) \leftrightarrow p]$ is always true.
(14) Modus ponens from (9) and (12).
(15) From (12) and (14), as $[(p \leftrightarrow q) \wedge (q \leftrightarrow r)] \leftrightarrow (p \leftrightarrow r)$ is always true.
(16) Definition of $\notin$.
(17) A contradiction, because $p \leftrightarrow \neg p$ is always false.

The reader is invited to treat the theory of equivalence (see 1.22) himself by means of symbols.

Functions

3.22 | In 1.11 we considered the terminology for mappings and functions. Notations such as

1) the function $f(x)$,
2) the function $y = f(x)$,
3) the function $x^2 - 3x + 2$,
4) the function $y = x^2 - 3x + 2$,
5) the function $ax^2 + bx + c$

are objectionable and will eventually drop out of use. The objections to them will be illustrated with the aid of some examples.
1) In the sentence "The function $f(x)$ assumes the value $f(a)$ for $x = a$" $f(x)$ is evidently meant to be a function and $f(a)$ a number. Why? The letter a is no better and no worse than the letter x.
2) If $y = f(x)$ is a function, then $y - f(x) = 0$ must, according to the rules of algebra, be the same function. Now consider for example $f(x) = 2x$. Then $y - 2x = 0$ must therefore be a function. But which function? Must x perforce be the "independent" and y the "dependent" variable?
3) This notation is the least disputable. Only, it will not get us very far. Instead of the second-degree polynomial, take for example x or 7. We must then speak of the function x and of the function 7. This is in itself already not too nice. But, in addition, the terminology 3) leads directly to the terminology 5) which is unsatisfactory for other reasons.

4) This is open to the same objection as 3).
5) What is meant is that this is a function of x. Why? Why not a function of a, b or c or all of them?
In physics a function which is derived from "the function $f(x)$" by substituting for x "the function $\varphi(t)$" is very frequently referred to as "the function $f(t)$". This is very confusing.
The correct terminology is illustrated by the following examples:

The equation

$$f(x) = 3x^2 - 6x - 9 \quad \text{(for all } x)$$

defines a function (mapping) f.
The equation

$$f(x) = 3x^2 - 6x - 9 \quad \text{(for all } x \text{ with } 0 < x < 1)$$

defines a function f which maps the set of the x with $0 < x < 1$ onto the set of the x with $-12 < x < -9$.
The equation

$$\sin x = x - \frac{x^3}{3!} + \frac{x^5}{5!} - \dots$$

defines the function sin (the sine function).
$3x^2 - 6x - 9$ as a function of x is continuous.
If by f we understand the expression $3x^2 - 6x - 9$ as a function of x, then $f(x) = 3x^2 - 6x - 9$.
$ax^2 + bx + c$ as a function of x is a quadratic function of x for all $a \neq 0$.

A precise terminology for functions (mappings) is especially necessary if sets of functions are considered. How should we write down, that a function is a member of a set A? If we designate the function by $f(x)$, then this membership should be denoted by something like $f(x) \in A$. But $f(x) \in A$ has an entire different meaning, namely that the value, which f assigns to x, is a member of A. The notation $f \in A$ however is completely unobjectionable. Something similar occurs, if a set of functions is mapped into another (or the same) set. For example, let $K(s, t)$ be continuous as a function of the pair $\ulcorner s, t \urcorner$ $(0 \leq s \leq 1, 0 \leq t \leq 1)$. The equation

$$g(s) = \int_0^1 K(s, t) f(t) \, dt$$

defines a mapping A with

$$Af = g.$$

A maps the set of the continuous functions (defined in the interval from 0 to 1) into itself. A can also be defined by

$$(Af)(s) = \int_0^1 K(s, t)f(t)\,dt$$

(for all s with $0 \leq s \leq 1$ and all continuous f defined in the interval from 0 to 1). It would here be meaningless to speak of

$$Af(t) = g(s).$$

The variables s and t have nothing to do with f, g and A. The mapping A acts upon f as a whole and produces the total g as image. (Yet such senseless notations are still often encountered in the literature.)

Only for a few functions, such as sin, cos, log, are fixed symbols available. There is no fixed function symbol for

$$3x^2 - 6x - 9 \text{ as a function of } x.$$

We can introduce a name f for this function by means of the definition

$$\bigwedge_x [f(x) = 3x^2 - 6x - 9].$$

But language becomes an unwieldy instrument if we must devise a name *ad hoc* for every particular thing. It is a gratifying feature of the language of mathematics that it has algorithmic names for most things, i.e., names which are formed according to definite rules. (Think of the natural numbers with their names formed by such rules.)

$$3x^2 - 6x - 9 \text{ as a function of } x$$

is an algorithmic name for the function in question, but this name is too cumbersome. We will shorten this a little and therefore write

$$\Upsilon_x(3x^2 - 6x - 9).$$

Hence this means: $3x^2 - 6x - 9$ as a function of x.

If we do not wish to consider such a function for all values of x, but solely in a set A, then we shall write this A behind the expression which determines the function value, and separated by a dotted vertical. Hence

$$\Upsilon_x(3x^2 - 6x - 9 \mid \uparrow_x - 3 < x < 5)$$

denotes a function which is defined only in the interval from -3 to 5.

$$\Upsilon_x(ax^2 + bx + c)$$

yields, for every value of a, b, c, a function;

$$\curlyvee_{\lceil x,a,b,c\rceil}(ax^2+bx+c)$$

on the other hand, is a function of the quartet of variables x, a, b, c. Of course:

$$\curlyvee_x f(x)=f.$$
$$(\curlyvee_x f(x))(a)=f(a).$$

If x runs over a set A and y over a set B — i.e., $\lceil x, y\rceil$ in $\lceil A, B\rceil$ — then

$$\curlyvee_x\curlyvee_y f(x,y),$$
$$\curlyvee_y\curlyvee_x f(x,y),$$
$$\curlyvee_{\lceil x,y\rceil} f(x,y)$$

are generally different things. Indeed for $a \in A$

$$(\curlyvee_x\curlyvee_y f(x,y))(a)=\curlyvee_y f(a,y),$$

whereas

$$(\curlyvee_y\curlyvee_x f(x,y))(a)\quad\text{and}\quad(\curlyvee_{\lceil x,y\rceil} f(x,y))(a)$$

will generally be meaningless. In fact in these functions only elements of B and $\lceil A, B\rceil$, respectively, are allowed to be substituted for the variable. Similarly holds for $b \in B$

$$(\curlyvee_y\curlyvee_x f(x,y))(b)=\curlyvee_x f(x,b),$$

whereas

$$(\curlyvee_x\curlyvee_y f(x,y))(b)\quad\text{and}\quad(\curlyvee_{\lceil x,y\rceil} f(x,y))(b)$$

will generally be meaningless.

3.23 | Just like

$$x^2-6x-9$$

we can conceive

  x is a man

as a function of x. In the former case the set of images (or *range*) consists of numbers; in the latter case it consists of propositions. The second function can be designated by

  ... is a man.

If we fill in the dots, we obtain a proposition. This function therefore maps the set of subjects into the set of the propositions. This is known as a propositional function. With the abbreviation introduced in the previous section this function can also be denoted by

$$\curlyvee_x \quad (x \text{ is a man}).$$

The relation

... smaller than ...

can similarly be denoted by

$$\curlyvee_{\ulcorner x,y \urcorner}(x < y).$$

3.24 | *Problems*

Give symbolic expressions for the following functions (predicates):
1. The square of ...
2. The square root of ...
3. The set of subsets of ...
4. The mother of ...
5. What I see (as a function of time).
6. The relation "being married".
7. The uncle–nephew relation.
8. What is $[\curlyvee_{\ulcorner a,b,c \urcorner} \uparrow_x (ax^2 + bx + c = 0)] \ulcorner 1, -3, 2 \urcorner$?
9. Compare $\curlyvee_x(x > 0)$ and $\uparrow_x(x > 0)$.
10. What is the meaning of $\curlyvee_f f(1) \ \vdots \ f \in [(\uparrow_x(x > 0)) \frown (\uparrow_x(x > -3))]$?
11. What is the meaning of $\uparrow_f(\wedge_{x,y}[f(x + y) = f(x) + f(y)])$?
12. Write down a symbolic expression for the function which is 0 for all instants t at which I see nothing and which is 1 for all instants t at which I do see something.

Binding

3.25 | To distinguish modern logic from the older logic that was studied since Aristotle's day, the term "logistics" is often employed. Its founders were G. PEANO (1858 or 1859–1932), WHITEHEAD (1861–1947) and BERTRAND RUSSELL (1872–...). The language of logistics differs from everyday speech in the way it treats the variables. "Dog" is a variable in the sentences

> There goes a dog.
> A dog is a mammal.

In the first sentence the variable "dog" has been bound existentially (there is a dog that goes there); in the second it has been bound in a generalizing manner (every dog is a mammal). This is not apparent from the form: it is inferred from the contents.

In everyday language the variables are highly specialized. The variable "dog" can be used only for dogs, the variable "cat" only for cats, the variable "something" only for things, the variable "somebody" only for persons (sometimes also for animals), the variable "somewhere" only for places, etc. In all these variables often no formal distinction is made between existential binding and generalizing binding. Consider also the examples

> I have eaten something.
> Something is better than nothing.

In cases where a number of variables of the same kind are required, difficulties are readily encountered in ordinary speech. We speak of "a dog" and "another dog", of "this dog" and "that dog". Already in ancient times the geometricians felt the need for a large number of variables to indicate points. As long as geometry was taught verbally, it was possible to manage with variables such as "this point" and "that point"; in order to record that science more precisely in writing, the point variables were defined by "point A", "point B", "point C", etc. From this originated our practice of indicating variables by letters. In logistic language the variables are, in general, freely interchangeable. The way of binding a variable is accurately indicated. We have, in the foregoing, been introduced to:

binding by substitution (see 3.3),
existential binding ($\vee$),
generalizing binding ($\wedge$),
binding by the article ($\downarrow$),
set forming binding ($\uparrow$),
function forming binding ($\curlyvee$).

In all these operations the variability of the variable vanishes.
In ordinary speech there is another, very important form of binding, namely, the

demonstrative binding.

"Here" is a place variable which, as a result of being uttered, is bound to the

place where it is uttered; "now" is a time variable which, as a result of being uttered, is bound to the instant at which it is uttered; "I" is bound by the speaker to himself. The same thing applies to "there", "yesterday", "you", "this", "that", etc. These variables are bound "demonstratively".
The last binding that we shall consider is the

interrogative binding,

which is symbolized by a question mark.

3.26 | "Find the x which satisfies $3x = 4$" is written as

$$?_x(3x = 4).$$

In

$$?_x(x^2 - 3x + 2 = 0)$$

we ask for all solutions of the equation.

3.27 | Problems

1. Write down: For which b are there values of a such that $-x^2 + ax + a + b$ is negative for all x?
Let $F(x, y, t, p)$ signify: x makes the statement p to y at the instant t. Write down:
2. When did x say something to himself?
3. What will someone, when it is told to him, never repeat to anyone else?
4. How much later is something, that some one tells, told back to him?
5. Who tells everyone what I have seen?

4.1 | So far, we have concerned ourselves with an efficient logical symbolism. We have described a *language*, the logistic language. Occasionally we also worked in this language. We have drawn symbolic conclusions and we have constructed conclusion chains and proofs. We went about it rather unsystematically. Of course, it is useful in itself to establish that something can be derived from something else. But if we are to systematize it, we must start with a system of assertions and thereafter derive everything, directly or indirectly, from these assertions.

Such preliminary assertions are called *axioms*, and we speak of the *axiomatic method* if a branch of mathematics (or some other science) is so organized that out of all true assertions a group is selected from which all other true assertions relating to that branch or subject can be derived.

A classic example of the axiomatic method is afforded by the axioms of geometry. In natural space we came to know certain properties of those things which we call points, lines, planes, circles, etc. A few of these assertions are chosen as axioms. Are there sufficient (and the right ones), then it is possible to derive from them all desired geometric assertions without once having to refer back to physical space. Indeed, we can completely forget the meanings of such words as point, line, etc.

4.2 | Example: P is a set of things, called *points*. Certain subsets of P are named *lines*. Let R denote the set of lines. Certain subsets of P are called *planes*, while V denotes the set of planes. We postulate:

1. $\bigwedge_{p,q}\{[(p \in P) \wedge (q \in P)] \to \bigvee_r[(r \in R) \wedge (p \in r) \wedge (q \in r)]\}$.

2. $\bigwedge_{p,q,r,s}\{[(p \in P) \wedge (q \in P) \wedge (r \in R) \wedge (s \in R) \wedge (p \in r \cap s) \wedge$
$\qquad\qquad (q \in r \cap s)] \to [(p = q) \vee (r = s)]\}$.

3. $\bigwedge_{p,q,r}\{[(p \in P) \wedge (q \in P) \wedge (r \in P)]$
$\qquad\qquad \to \bigvee_v[(v \in V) \wedge (p \in v) \wedge (q \in v) \wedge (r \in v)]\}$.

4. $\bigwedge_{p,q,r,v,w}([(p \in P) \wedge (q \in P) \wedge (r \in P) \wedge (v \in V) \wedge (w \in V) \wedge$
$\qquad (p \in v \cap w) \wedge (q \in v \cap w) \wedge (r \in v \cap w)] \to$
$\qquad\qquad \{(v = w) \vee \bigvee_s [(s \in R) \wedge (p \in s) \wedge (q \in s) \wedge (r \in s)]\})$.

5. $\bigwedge_{p,q,r,v}\{[(p \in P) \wedge (q \in P) \wedge (r \in R) \wedge (v \in V) \wedge (p \in r) \wedge (q \in r) \wedge$
$\qquad\qquad (p \in v) \wedge (q \in v)] \to [(p = q) \vee (r \subset v)]\}$.

6. $\bigwedge_{p,v,w}\{[(p \in P) \wedge (v \in V) \wedge (w \in V) \wedge (p \in v \cap w)] \to$
$\qquad\qquad \bigvee_r[(r \in R) \wedge (r \subset v \cap w)]\}$.

A substantial portion of geometry is derivable from these axioms. To do this, it is not necessary to know *what* points, lines and planes are.

For example, derive the assertion: One, and only one, plane can pass through a line and a point located outside that line. Two different planes have no point or an entire line in common.

The beginning of this section could have been phrased somewhat more precisely:

By an incidence geometry we understand a triplet $\ulcorner P, R, V \urcorner$ so that

$$(r \in R) \rightarrow (r \subset P),$$
$$(v \in V) \rightarrow (v \subset P)$$

holds and the requirements 1–6 are met.

4.3 | As a matter of fact, we already encountered axiomatic systems of this kind in earlier sections of this book. For instance, from the axioms for the equivalence concept, namely,

$$\wedge_a (a \sim a),$$
$$\wedge_{a,b,c} \{[(b \sim a) \wedge (c \sim a)] \rightarrow (c \sim b)\}$$

we can derive all assertions concerning the equivalence concept which we regard as being generally true.

Similarly, from

$$\wedge_{a,b} \{(a \neq b) \leftrightarrow [(a < b) \vee (b < a)]\}$$
$$\wedge_{a,b} [(a < b) \rightarrow \neg(b < a)]$$
$$\wedge_{a,b,c} \{[(a < b) \wedge (b < c) \rightarrow (a < c)]\}$$

we can derive all the general properties of the concept of order. If necessary, we can further add the definitions

$$\wedge_{a,b} [(a > b) \leftrightarrow (b < a)],$$
$$\wedge_{a,b} \{(a \leqq b) \leftrightarrow [(a < b) \vee (a = b)]\},$$

etc.

If we draw up a system of axioms, we have to take care that there does not follow too much or too little from these axioms (in particular no false assertions).

4.4 | We now wish to set up a system of axioms for the calculus of propositions. In doing this we shall go further than in the previous examples. We shall not only indicate precisely the propositions (axioms) from which we shall start, but also the manner of deriving from these axioms new assertions that are to be regarded as true. In the previous examples it was tacitly supposed that this would have to be effected by means of the well known logical methods. What those well known logical methods actually are, was not explicitly agreed upon. We shall now, however, indicate precisely which operations may be applied directly, or indirectly, to the axioms in order to obtain assertions that are to be regarded as true, i.e. *theorems*. Also, we shall indicate precisely how proper formulae may look. ("→*p*→", for example, is not a proper formula.)

Our formulae have no meaning at all, nor will the letters and arrows which occur in them have any meaning. They are merely a set of marks on paper. The reader is expected to be able to distinguish and identify them. If two arrows fortuitously differ a little in appearance, he will nevertheless have to identify them as similar symbols. All operations will be *formalized*. A machine should be able to perform them.

However, afterwards, we shall again interpret the marks made on the paper; the *theorems* have to correspond to the always-true propositions.

Among the symbols used in the following

$$\rightarrow \quad \text{and} \quad \otimes$$

play a leading part. In the case of "→" we keep in mind its usual meaning. "$\otimes$" will later be interpreted as an always false proposition. The two above-mentioned symbols are "constant", as contrary to $p, q, r, \ldots$, which are "variable", i.e., for which something else may be substituted.

4.5 | *Axioms for Propositions*

The *propositional language* is composed of

primitive formulae*)   ($\otimes, p, q, r, \ldots$)

and

connectives: → (arrow), (,) (parentheses).

Formulae:

a) every primitive formula is a formula,

b) if A and B are formulae, then $(A \rightarrow B)$ is also a formula,

c) all formulae are derivable from primitive formulae by repeated application of the principle (b).

Comments: The A and B mentioned above are not products of the propositional

---

*) "Primitive" because compound formulae are built up from them.

language with which we are here concerned. They are rather abbreviations for more or less complex products of that language.

Instead of $A \to \otimes$ we will also write $\neg A$. We do not need $\vee$ and $\wedge$ for they can essentially be expressed in $\to$ and $\neg$.

For convenience we shall omit the outermost parentheses, and for additional clarity we shall also use braces and square brackets.

Axioms: If A, B and C are formulae, then

1. $C \to (A \to C)$,
2. $(A \to B) \to \{[A \to (B \to C)] \to (A \to C)\}$,
3. $(\neg(\neg A)) \to A$

are axioms.

Monus ponens is an operation whereby from two formulae

$$A$$

and $A \to B$

the formula B

is obtained.

If Γ is a set of formulae and D is a formula, then we understand by

Proof of D from Γ a chain of formulae with D as the last formula, in such a manner that each link of that chain is
(a) either an axiom
(b) or taken from Γ,
(c) or obtained by modus ponens from an appropriate pair of previous links in that chain.

Provable from Γ is said of a formula D if there is a proof of D from Γ. To denote this we use the symbol

$\Gamma \vdash D$.

Γ-theorem is any formula which is provable from Γ.
Γ-theory is the set of all formulae provable from Γ.
If Γ is empty, then we simply speak of *provable, theorem, theory.*

$\vdash D$

means: D is provable.

4.6 | Deduction Theorem

If

$$\Gamma, A \vdash D.$$

then also

$$\Gamma \vdash A \to D.$$

Proof*): The supposition states that there is a proof of D from Γ, A. This proof is a sequence of formulae, Σ. We replace each link C of that chain Σ by $A \to C$. We thus obtain a new chain Σ'. The last member of that chain will then be $A \to D$, i.e., that which, according to the assertion, should be provable from Γ. However Σ' is not yet a proof. We must insert some additional links. Corresponding to the definition of "proof from Γ" we have to distinguish the following cases for the links of Σ (see 4.5, "proof of D from Γ").

(a) C is an axiom,
(b) C is taken from Γ, A,
     (b') C is taken from Γ,
     (b'') C is A,
(c) C has been obtained from previous links of Σ by means of modus ponens.

(a) Before the link $A \to C$ in Σ' we insert the axioms

$$C, C \to (A \to C)$$

(See axioms 1.). $A \to C$ is obtained from this by modus ponens.

(b') Before $A \to C$ in Σ' we insert the links

$$C, C \to (A \to C),$$

of which the first is taken from Γ and the second is an axiom. $A \to C$ is again obtained by modus ponens.

(b'') By substituting A for C in axioms 2, we obtain the axiom

$$(A \to B) \to \{[A \to (B \to A)] \to (A \to A)\}.$$

By substituting $A \to A$ for B, we obtain from this axiom the axiom

$$(A \to (A \to A)) \to \{[A \to ((A \to A) \to A)] \to (A \to A)\}. \tag{1}$$

---

*) Note that this word "proof" has a different meaning from the one used before. There it denoted a formal operation within the propositional language, but here it has the usual meaning.

Before $A \to A$ we now insert in Σ' this axiom, furthermore the axiom

$$A \to (A \to A) \tag{2}$$

obtained from axioms 1 with C instead of A and

$$[A \to ((A \to A) \to A)] \to (A \to A), \tag{3}$$

which is obtained from (1), (2) by modus ponens, furthermore the axiom

$$A \to ((A \to A) \to A) \tag{4}$$

also obtained from axioms 1 with A instead of C and with $A \to A$ instead of A. Then finally $A \to A$ is obtained from (3) and (4) by modus ponens.

(c) Let C have been obtained by modus ponens from

$$B \tag{5}$$
$$B \to C, \tag{6}$$

which occur before C in Σ. In Σ' the corresponding formulae are

$$A \to B, \tag{5'}$$
$$A \to (B \to C), \tag{6'}$$

which therefore occur before the $A \to C$ under consideration.
Before this $A \to C$ insert: axiom 2

$$(A \to B) \to \{[A \to (B \to C)] \to (A \to C)\}, \tag{7}$$

and furthermore

$$[A \to (B \to C)] \to (A \to C), \tag{8}$$

which follows from (5') and (7) by modus ponens.
Then

$$A \to C$$

is justified at its place by modus ponens from (6') and (8).
With all these insertions Σ' has become a proof of $A \to D$ from Γ, as was our intention.

4.7 | A few more theorems.

(6) $\vdash (\neg B) \to (B \to C)$.

Proof: Axioms 1 include

$$\otimes \to (A \to \otimes)$$

or with a different notation

$$\otimes \to (\neg A).$$

Hence also (with $\neg C$ instead of A):

$$\otimes \to (\neg(\neg C)).$$

Hence $\otimes \vdash \neg(\neg C)$.

$$(\neg(\neg C)) \to C$$

belongs to axioms 3.

$$\neg(\neg C), (\neg(\neg C)) \to C, C$$

is a proof of C from $\otimes$. Hence

$$\otimes \vdash C$$

From the false $\otimes$ follows everything.
Therefore (deduction theorem)

$$\vdash \otimes \to C.$$

Hence there is a proof for $\otimes \to C$. Henceforth we may include $\otimes \to C$ in proof chains: if desired, the proof for $\otimes \to C$ can be inserted beforehand.

From $B \to \otimes$, B a proof for C is

$$\otimes, \otimes \to C, C.$$

Hence

$$B \to \otimes, B \vdash C.$$

Hence (deduction theorem)

$$B \to \otimes \vdash B \to C,$$

and therefore (again applying the deduction theorem)

$$\vdash (B \to \otimes) \to (B \to C),$$

which was to be proved.

(7) $\vdash B \to [(\neg C) \to (\neg(B \to C))].$

Proof: $B, \neg C, B \to C \vdash C, C \to \otimes, \otimes.$

Hence (deduction theorem)

$$B, \neg C \vdash (B \to C) \to \otimes,$$

(again): $B \vdash (\neg C) \rightarrow (\neg(B \rightarrow C))]$,
(again): $\vdash B \rightarrow [(\neg C) \rightarrow (\neg(B \rightarrow C))]$.

4.8 | In the proof of 6 from 4.7 we encountered

$\quad \otimes \vdash C$

and

$\quad \vdash \otimes \rightarrow C.$

Hence: if $\otimes$ is in Γ, then the Γ-theory consists of *all* formulae. Stated more generally: if $\otimes$ is provable from Γ, then every formula is provable from Γ. A theory of this kind is not interesting. We prefer theories in which not every formula is provable. We call
Γ *consistent* if $\otimes$ is not provable from Γ or — what amounts to the same thing — if not every formula is provable from Γ.
If Γ is consistent, then not both A and $\neg A$ can be provable from Γ, because: with A and $A \rightarrow \otimes$ also $\otimes$ would be provable, so that Γ would be inconsistent.
If Γ is consistent and $\Gamma \vdash A$, then Γ, A is also consistent, because otherwise $\Gamma, A \vdash \otimes$, hence (deduction theorem) $\Gamma \vdash A \rightarrow \otimes$, and therefore both A and $\neg A$ would be provable from Γ.
If Γ is consistent, then either Γ, A or $\Gamma, \neg A$ is consistent. Otherwise $\Gamma, A \vdash \otimes$ as well as $\Gamma, \neg A \vdash \otimes$, hence $\Gamma \vdash \neg A$ as well as $\Gamma \vdash \neg(\neg A)$, and therefore $\Gamma \vdash A$.
A consistent Γ can be extended to a

$\quad$ *maximally consistent Γ,*

i.e., to a set of formulae which, with any further extension, becomes inconsistent. To this end, we shall conceive all the formulae as being arranged in a row in accordance with some appropriate ordering principle*).
We seek the first formula which is not yet in Γ and which can be added to Γ without disturbing the consistency. We add this formula to Γ. Continuing in this way, we obtain a set Δ of formulae which comprises Γ and to which, on penalty of inconsistency, no further formula can be added. From the foregoing follows:
If Δ is maximally consistent, then precisely one member of the pair A, $\neg A$ will belong to Δ, and everything that is provable from Δ will belong to Δ.

---

*) This is directly possible if the language in question has only a countable number of primitive formulae, and therefore also only a countable number of formulae. The reader should bear this case in mind. In general, the desired object can be achieved with what is known as a well-ordering of the formulae. This cannot be dealt with here.

Valuation of the Propositional Language

4.9 | In the foregoing it was already announced that we were going to interpret the propositional language. This is what we shall do now. We shall "valuate" the formulae. We speak of a

Valuation of the propositional language if to each formula precisely one of the "values" 0 (false) or 1 (true) is so assigned that $\otimes$ has the value 0 and for each pair of formulae B, C the value of $B \to C$ is determined by the table of values

B	C	$B \to C$
0	0	1
0	1	1
1	0	0
1	1	1

In a valuation all axioms (see 4.5) *automatically have the value 1.*

Proof:

Axioms (1) can have the value 0 only if $A \to C$ has the value 0 and C has the value 1; but these two are contradictory.

(2) can have the value 0 only if the successive values are

$A \to B$	1
$(A \to (B \to C)) \to (A \to C)$	0
$A \to (B \to C)$	1
$A \to C$	0
A	1
C	0
B	1 (because of 1st and 5th line)
$B \to C$	0 (because of 6th and 7th line)
A	0 (because of 3rd and 8th line).

But then there is a contradiction between the 5th and 9th line.

(3) can have the value 0 only if A has the value 0 and $(A \to \otimes) \to \otimes$ has the value 1; but then $A \to \otimes$ on the one hand has the value 0, and on the other hand has the value 1.

In a valuation all theorems have the value 1.

For let D be a theorem and C be a link of a proof for D. Let us furthermore suppose that all the links preceding C have the value 1. We need only show that this is also true for C. If C is an axiom, then C has the value 1 (as proved in the foregoing); if C has been obtained by means of modus ponens from earlier

B, $B \to C$ having the value 1, then the table of values shows that C must also have the value 1.

In accordance with 2.4 we call a set of formulae Γ

satisfiable if there is a valuation for which all formulae from Γ obtain the value 1; a valuation of this kind is called a satisfaction of Γ. If there is no such a valuation, then Γ is said to be

unsatisfiable or *false*.

A formula A is said to be

Γ-*true* if, for *every* valuation, which is a satisfaction of Γ, A gets the value 1. A is called

true (pure and simple) if A gets the value 1 for *every* valuation. If, for some valuations, A gets the value 0, then A is therefore not true and is accordingly said to be

disputable.

"True" and "indisputable" are therefore the same thing.

For each valuation A and $\neg A$ have different values, because, according to the table of values for $A \to B$, the value 1 would follow for $\otimes$ from equal values for A and $A \to \otimes$, and this is contradictory to the definition of valuation.

Hence it follows that:

If A is true, then $\neg A$ is false. If A is false, then $\neg A$ is true.

4.10 | Every language has a *syntactic* aspect and a *semantic* aspect. If we translate the French "il pleut" by "he is raining" or by "it are raining", we are committing a syntactic error. If we translate it by "it is snowing", we are committing a semantic error (though it is syntactically correct). Syntax is concerned with the formal aspects of a language, whereas semantics is concerned with meanings. "Verb", "endings", "sentence", "punctuation mark" are syntactic concepts. "Synonym", "metaphor", "a carefully worded statement", "true" are semantic concepts.

In 4.5–8 we were concerned with syntactic matters. In 4.9 we were in the field of semantics. By evaluating formulae we give them a meaning; the values 0,1 have nothing to do with the vocabulary of the propositional language. "Formula", "proof", "provable", "consistent" did not, it is true, belong to the propositional language either but had been defined on the basis of that language; they correspond to concepts such as "verb", "endings", "sentence", "punctuation mark" with regard to ordinary language. "Satisfiable", "false", "true" "disputable" correspond to "synonym", etc. To be on the safe side we accordingly say *semantically* true or false if these concepts are meant; the syntactic truth aspect is provability.

4.11 | Let Γ be a satisfiable set of formulae. Let D be provable from Γ. For each satisfaction of Γ, D gets the value 1.
This can be shown as follows. For a link C of the proof of D there are three possibilities, namely, C is

a)   an axiom,
b)   taken from Γ,
c)   obtained by modus ponens from two preceding links of the proof:

  $B, B \to C$.

For case a) we know from 4.9 that C has the value 1, and in case b) C will have the value 1 by definition of valuation and satisfaction of Γ. If we already know that all the links of the proof preceding C have the value 1, then we know this more particularly for B and $B \to C$. The table of values for $B \to C$ shows that C must then also have the value 1. Each link is therefore a formula with the value 1. Hence D, as the last link, must also have the value 1.

4.12 | *Every satisfiable Γ is consistent.*

For, according to 4.11, everything provable from Γ has the value 1. Now $\otimes$ has the value 0 and is therefore not provable from Γ. Hence Γ is consistent. The reverse of this theorem is also true:

Every consistent Γ is satisfiable.

Proof: According to 4.8 we determine for Γ a maximally consistent Δ which comprises Γ. Furthermore, according to 4.8, of each pair $A, \neg A$ precisely one is in Δ.
To all members of Δ we assign the value 1, to all non-members we assign the value 0. We shall verify that this is a valuation.
$\otimes$ has the value 0, for because of the consistency of Δ, $\otimes$ does not belong to Δ.
Now check the table values (4.9):
In the case of the first two lines, $\neg B$ is in Δ; since theorem 6 (from 4.7) is in Δ, we have $\Delta \vdash (B \to C)$; hence $B \to C$ is in Δ, so $B \to C$ does indeed have the value 1. In the case of the third line, B is in Δ and $\neg C$ is in Δ; since theorem 7 (from 4.7) is in Δ, we have $\Delta \vdash \neg(B \to C)$; hence $\neg(B \to C)$ in Δ, and so $B \to C$

is indeed not in $\varDelta$; hence $B \rightarrow C$ has the value 0. In the case of the second and the fourth line, C is in $\varDelta$; since $C \rightarrow (B \rightarrow C)$ occurs among the axioms 1, we have $\varDelta \vdash B \rightarrow C$, and therefore $B \rightarrow C$ is in $\varDelta$; hence $B \rightarrow C$ has really the value 1.

Thus $\varGamma$ is satisfied, for $\varDelta$ contains $\varGamma$ and every formula in $\varDelta$ gets the value 1.

4.13 | By contraposition we obtain from the previous theorem:

> *Every unsatisfiable (false) $\varGamma$ is inconsistent.*

We now arrive at the main result, the

> THEOREM OF COMPLETENESS: *In propositional language every true formula is provable.*

Proof: Let A be true. Then $\neg A$ is false (see end of 4.9) and therefore unsatisfiable and — by virtue of the previous theorem — inconsistent. Hence

$$\neg A \vdash \otimes$$

and therefore

$$\vdash (\neg A) \rightarrow \otimes.$$

We now successively write down:

> a proof for $\neg(\neg A)$, axiom 3, A.

This is a proof for A. Hence A is provable.

This theorem shows that our set of axioms is adequate for proving any true formula.

This explains why it is called the "completeness theorem".

Axioms of the Subject-Predicate Language

4.14 | The propositional language so far considered in this chapter is a rather poor language. In the third chapter we were introduced to much more powerful linguistic resources. These will now be subjected to axiomatization. A

Subject-predicate language
is composed of

Subjects among which an infinite number of *variable* and (perhaps also, but not necessarily) *constant* subjects,

Primitive*) predicates, of degree 0, 1, 2, ..., which must include the 0th-degree predicate $\otimes$ (the 0th-degree predicates are what we formerly called primitive formulae — propositions),

Connectives: $\rightarrow$, (,) , $\wedge$.
The subjects and predicates together are called the vocabulary of the language.

Formulae:
a) If f is a primitive predicate of degree $n > 0$ and if $x_1, \ldots, x_n$ are subjects, then $f(x_1, \ldots, x_n)$ is a formula. Every primitive predicate of degree 0 is a formula.
b) If A and B are formulae, then $(A \rightarrow B)$ is also a formula.
c) If A is a formula and x is a variable subject, then $\wedge_x A$ is a formula.
d) All formulae are obtainable by repeated application of the principles a), b), c).
Instead of "variable subject" we may refer more briefly to "variable".

Free and bound variables.
Depending on the way — a), b), c) — in which a formula originates, we define the "free" or "bound" occurrence of a variable.
a) In $f(x_1, \ldots, x_n)$ the x_i (if it is a variable subject) occurs freely.
b) Any free or bound occurrence of the variable x in A (and similarly in B) is also called free or bound occurrence, respectively, in $A \rightarrow B$.
c) Any free or bound occurrence of a variable y in A is also called free or bound occurrence, respectively, in $\wedge_x A$ if the variable y differs from the variable x; any occurrence of the variable x in $\wedge_x A$ is called bound. (The presence of the x as subscript to $\wedge$ is not regarded as "occurrence".)
For any occurrence of a variable in an *arbitrary* formula it is, by means of these conventions, determined whether it must be regarded as free or as bound.
A formula with n different free variables is called a formula of degree n.
A formula of degree 0 is called a *proposition*.
We write $\neg A$ instead of $A \rightarrow \otimes$.

Axioms: If A, B, C are formulae, then the axioms are:

    1, 2, 3 (see 4.5),
    4. $\wedge_x(A \rightarrow B) \rightarrow (A \rightarrow \wedge_x B)$, if the variable x does not occur freely in A;
    5. $\wedge_x A \rightarrow A'$, if A' is obtained from A by substitution of a subject y for x wherever x occurs, while it is understood that x does not occur freely in any sub-formula of A of the form $\wedge_y C$.

---

*) See footnote p. 71.

Besides the

Modus ponens we shall here accept another means to establish a proof, namely,

Binding: an operation whereby a formula B is replaced by a formula $\wedge_x B$.

Proof of D from Γ is defined as in 4.5 with the addition
(d) or obtained by binding with $\wedge_x$ from a previous formula in that chain, while
it is understood that such an x does not freely occur in any formula of Γ.

Provable from Γ is then defined as in 4.5. The same applies to the concepts:

Γ-theorem, Γ-theory, provable, theorem, theory.
The proof of the

Deduction Theorem now requires a supplement, corresponding to the addition (d) to the definition of proof:
If

$$B, \wedge_x B$$

are links in a proof from Γ, A, then we have to insert extra links in this proof
between

$$A \to B, \quad A \to \wedge_x B.$$

As such we shall take

$$\wedge_x(A \to B),$$

which is obtained from $A \to B$ by binding, and the axiom

$$\wedge_x(A \to B) \to (A \to \wedge_x B).$$

(Note that x was not allowed to occur freely in Γ, A.) From these two formulae
we then obtain $A \to \wedge_x B$ by modus ponens.
We shall use the abbreviation

$$\vee_x A \quad \text{for} \quad \neg\wedge_x(\neg A).$$

The proofs of 6 and 7, as considered in 4.7 remain unchanged. One easily proves

(8) $\vdash \wedge_x(\neg A) \to (\neg\vee_x A)$.

(9) $\vdash \neg\wedge_x A \to \vee_x(\neg A)$.

Consistency is defined as in 4.8 .

4.15 | Formulae without free variables are called *propositions*, since with these
formulae we can do everything that was done with propositions in 4.5–13.

More particularly, we can extend every consistent set of propositions into a maximally consistent set of propositions, to which belongs exactly one proposition out of any pair of propositions A, $\neg A$. We are going to do more than this, however.

Our vocabulary need not contain a single constant subject. The predicates are, as it were, floating in the air; they do not refer to anything. It may occur that $\bigvee_x A$ is provable and there is nevertheless no "example" of "there is an x so that A" in the vocabulary, i.e., there is no fixed subject which, on being substituted for x, turns A into a provable formula. Now we shall enlarge on one hand the

vocabulary by the addition of *constant subjects* and on the other hand a

given consistent set Γ_0 of propositions by adding fresh propositions, with the aim that the set of propositions Ω eventually obtained shall be

maximally consistent and that

for every proposition $\bigvee_x A$ from Ω a constant subject a can be found in the vocabulary, so that the *formula A′*, which is obtained from A by substitution (according to axioms 5) of a for x, *likewise belongs to Ω.*

We shall construct such a Ω stepwise. We shall keep a supply of things in readiness which we shall gradually add to the vocabularly as constant subjects. To start with, we shall extend the given Γ_0 to a maximally consistent Δ_0 (see 4.8). We can conceive the propositions from Δ_0 arranged in a row and we take the first proposition of type $\bigvee_x A$ (where x is a variable and A is a formula). Then we take a thing a from the available supply, add it to the vocabulary as a constant subject, and add to Δ_0 the proposition $A′$ that is obtained from A by substitution of a for x (in all places where x is free). We can show that Δ_0 will then remain consistent:

Suppose that Δ_0, $A′$ is inconsistent, i.e.,

$$\Delta_0,\ A′ \vdash \otimes,$$

hence (deduction theorem)

$$\Delta_0 \vdash \neg A′.$$

In the proof Σ for $\neg A′$ from Δ_0 we shall replace a, wherever it occurs, by a variable y which does not occur in the proof (here the infinity of the number of variables is used). We assert that the new chain Σ^* is again a proof. To see why this is so, consider each link of the proof C that is changed into a formula C^* as a result of the substitution of y for a. Having regard to the list of means to execute a proof there are four possibilities:

a) C is an axiom,

b)　C has been taken from $\varDelta_0$,

c)　C has been obtained from previous formulae of $\varSigma$ by modus ponens,

d)　C has the form $\wedge_z B$ and has been obtained from previous B by binding.

C case b) cannot occur because a has played no part at all in the constitution of $\varDelta_0$. In the case a) it is evident that C^* is again an axiom, and also in the cases c) and d) we see at once that C^* is obtained by the same procedure from previous formulae of $\varSigma^*$ as that whereby C was obtained from corresponding formulae of $\varSigma$.

Hence also

$$\varDelta_0 \vdash \neg A'',$$

where A'' is derived from A' by substitution of y for a, i.e., from A by substitution of y for x in all places where x occurs freely.

By binding of y we then also obtain

$$\varDelta_0 \vdash \wedge_y(\neg A'')$$

and by virtue of axioms (5)

$$\varDelta_0 \vdash \neg A;$$

whence we obtain by binding of x

$$\varDelta_0 \vdash \wedge_x(\neg A),$$

or

$$\varDelta_0 \vdash (\vee_x A) \to \otimes,$$

which, in combination with the given

$$\varDelta_0 \vdash \vee_x A$$

would lead to the inconsistency of $\varDelta_0$.

This contradiction is a consequence of the assumption that $\varDelta_0, A'$ was inconsistent. Hence it follows that $\varDelta_0$ remains consistent after the addition of A'. A' is now inserted behind $\vee_x A$, in the sequence in which the propositions of $\varDelta_0$ were placed. We shall now seek the second proposition of the same type, say $\vee_y B$, take a thing b from the available supply, add it to the vocabulary as a constant subject, and add to $\varDelta_0, A'$ the proposition B' which is obtained from B by the substitution of b for y. In this operation the consistency is again preserved. Proceeding in this manner, this process yields a vocabulary and a consistent set $\varGamma_1$ with the property: for each formula of the type $\vee_z K$ in $\varGamma_1$ a constant subject k can be found in the vocabulary, so that K' (obtained by substitution of k for every free occurrence of z in K) belongs to $\varGamma_1$.

$\varGamma_1$ is again extended into a maximally consistent set $\varDelta_1$ of propositions; $\varDelta_1$ is treated as Δ_0; this leads to a Γ_2 with properties analogous to those of Γ_1, etc. The ultimate result is an extension of the vocabulary and an extension of Γ to Ω with the desired properties:

Ω is a maximally consistent set of propositions;

for every proposition $\bigvee_x A$ from Ω there is an "example" a of "there is an x so that A".

This property of Ω can also be formulated as follows:

Ω is a maximally consistent set of propositions;

if all the propositions obtained from the formula A by the substitution of any particular constant subject for x belong to Ω, then $\bigwedge_x A$ belongs to Ω.

To prove this, suppose that this were not so. Then, because of the *maximal* consistency of Ω, $\neg \bigwedge_x A$ would belong to Ω, and so would therefore $\bigvee_x(\neg A)$. There would then be a constant subject a so that $\neg A'$ belongs to Ω (where A' is derived from A by substitution of a for x). Because of the consistency of Ω however, A' would then certainly not belong to Ω, and this would be contrary to the supposition. — The converse can be proved in similar fashion.

4.16 | The problem of the interpretation of the subject-predicate language introduced axiomatically in 4.14 is solved in principle with the construction of Ω.

What do we mean by such an interpretation? We want the "subjects", "predicates", " $\rightarrow$ ", " $\wedge$ " of the given subject-predicate language to correspond to something that is in agreement with our ideas thereof, as envisaged in Chapter 3. The subjects present no problems. But what did we mean in Chapter 3 by a predicate? A predicate such as "... is a man" was completely given if, with regard to anything filled in at the place of the dots, it was fixed whether it would make the proposition, thus obtained, true or false. The predicate "... smaller than ..." was determined if it was settled for which pairs it would become true and for which pairs it would become false. An nth-degree predicate F was determined if, for every n-tuple of things $a_1, \ldots, a_n$, it was certain whether F would thereby be made true or false. An nth-degree predicate was therefore a mapping of the set of the n-tuples of things into the set consisting of the judgements "true" and "false" (also called 1 and 0 respectively). The said set of things will be noted by I; the notation I^n will be used for the set $\lceil I, \ldots, I \rceil$ of the n-tuples from I. Hence we shall speak of an *interpretation* of the given subject-predicate language if

> with every constant subject a is associated an element of I, called Ra,
> with every nth-degree predicate F is associated a mapping, called RF, of I^n into the set $(0,1)$.

In this way, to a formula $F(x_1,\ldots,x_n)$ corresponds an expression $(RF)(x_1,\ldots,x_n)$ which, on substitution of elements of I for $x_1,\ldots,x_n$, assumes the value 0 or 1. A substitution of elements of I for the subjects of the subject-predicate language will be called a *cover* ω. Hence ω is a mapping of the set of subjects into the set I.

The interpretation R should be chosen fixed, but we shall, of course, consider *all* covers that agree with the interpretation (i.e. the covers which map every *constant* subject according to the interpretation R).

We must, however, require something more of an interpretation. As before, we shall require that (the 0th-degree predicate) $\otimes$ always gets the value 0; furthermore, that for "$\rightarrow$" the table of values in 4.9 shall apply and shall do so for every cover, that is not in conflict with R. But now there is an additional requirement with regard to "$\wedge$". In Chapter 3 we meant by $\wedge_x A$ that A, for every substitution for x, is true. To conform to this we must now demand: If the interpreation of A has the value 1 for every cover, then the interpretation of $\wedge_x A$ will also have the value 1. If these requirements are fulfilled, we shall call the interpretation "valuable".

This analysis can now be summarized in a definition.

4.17 | Consider a given subject-predicate language.

Let I be a set, I^n the set $\lceil I, \ldots, I \rceil$ of the n-tuples from I, and I^0 a set consisting of one element i_0.

A *cover* is a mapping ω which associates with every subject an element of I. An *interpretation* over I is a mapping R with the following property:

to every constant subject corresponds an element of I,
to every primitive predicate of the nth degree corresponds a mapping of I^n into the set $(0, 1)$.

Let R be an interpretation.

The cover ω *agrees with* the interpretation R if ω and R are the same for every constant subject. The only covers ω that will be allowed are those which agree with R.

R is called *valuable* if with every cover ω, R causes a valuation; i.e. to each formula C is assigned a value $|C|_\omega = 0$ or 1 (dependent on ω) so that the following requirements are fulfilled:

a) If C is of the form $f(x_1, \ldots, x_n)$ (f being an nth-degree primitive predicate, and $x_1, \ldots, x_n$ being subjects), then:

$$|C|_\omega = (Rf)(\lceil \omega(x_1), \ldots, \omega(x_n) \rceil) \quad \text{for} \quad n > 0,$$
$$= (Rf)(i_0) \qquad\qquad \text{for} \quad n = 0,$$
$$|\otimes|_\omega = 0.$$

b) If C is of the form $(A \rightarrow B)$, then $|C|_\omega$ will depend on $|A|_\omega$ and $|B|_\omega$ according to the table of values in 4.9.

c) If C is of the form $\bigwedge_z A$, then $|C|_\omega = 1$ if, and only if, $|A|_{\omega'} = 1$ for every cover ω' which only differs from ω in z.

In view of the origin of the formulae (see 4.14) such a valuation is possible in not more than one way (if the interpretation R is given).

On verifying the cases a), b), c) we see:

The value of C in ω depends only upon what ω assigns to the variables that are free in C. More particularly, the value of a proposition does not depend on ω. But it does of course depend on the interpretation R.

Let Γ be a set of propositions. A valuable interpretation over I, in which every proposition from Γ gets the value 1, is called a

satisfaction of Γ over I. If Γ has such a satisfaction, then Γ is said to be *satisfiable* over I; otherwise it is said to be

unsatisfiable or false over I.

A proposition A is said to be

Γ-*true over I* if, for each satisfaction of Γ over I, it gets the value 1,
Γ-*true* if it is Γ-true over I for every I,
true over I if, for every valuable interpretation over I, it gets the value 1,
true if, for every I, it is true over I.
"*Disputable*", etc. can be defined similarly.

4.18 | Let Γ be a set of propositions satisfiable over I. Let D be provable from Γ. For each satisfaction of Γ over I, D gets the value 1.

This is analogous to the theorem in 4.11 and it is proved in the same fashion. We must only take into account the possibility that the link C has been obtained from a preceding link by binding, i.e. it has the form $\bigwedge_x B$. If it is known of the links preceding C that they have the value 1 for the valuable interpretation R and every cover ω that agrees with R, then this will be known more particularly for B. According to the definition of a valuable interpretation (see 4.17c), $\bigwedge_x B$ will then also have the value 1 for every cover.

4.19 | Hence it follows (see also 4.12):

Every set of propositions that is satisfiable over a suitable I is consistent. The reverse of this is also valid:

Every consistent set of propositions is satisfiable over a suitable I.

Proof: We extend the set of the constant subjects and the given consistent system of propositions Γ according to 4.15. We obtain a maximally consistent system of propositions Ω which comprises Γ and in which, for every proposition $\bigvee_x A$, a constant subject a of the enriched language is to be found, so that the formula A', derived from A by substitution of a for x, also belongs to Ω.

For I we shall take the set of the constant subjects of the enriched language. The interpretation R is defined:

for every constant subject a we have

$$Ra = a,$$

for every primitive predicate f of degree n and every $\ulcorner a_1, \ldots a_n \urcorner$ from I^n we have

$$(Rf)(\ulcorner a_1, \ldots, a_n \urcorner) = 1 \text{ or } 0,$$

depending on whether from $f(x_1, \ldots, x_n)$, after substitution of a_i for $x_i (i = 1, \ldots, n)$, a proposition arises which does or does not belong to Ω.

R is valuable and $|C|_\omega$ is defined for every formula C, and for every cover ω agreeing with R, by the definition

$$|C|_\omega = 1 \text{ or } 0,$$

depending on whether, on substitution of $\omega(x)$ for every variable x that is free in C, from C a proposition is obtained which does or does not belong to Ω. To see this, we must only verify that the requirements a), b), c) in 4.17 are met.

a) Let C be of the form $f(x_1, \ldots, x_n)$ (see 4.17), $n > 0$. According to definition, $(Rf)(\ulcorner \omega(x_1), \ldots, \omega(x_n) \urcorner)$ is calculated by substituting $\omega(x_i)$ for x_i in $f(x_1, \ldots, x_n)$ and checking whether or not the result belongs to Ω. But according to the definition this is exactly the same as the calculation of $|f(x_1, \ldots, x_n)|_\omega$.

For $n = 0$ this is also evident. $|\otimes|_\omega = 0$ follows from the consistency of Ω (i.e., $\otimes$ not in Ω).

b) See the proof in 4.11.

c) Let C be of the form $\bigwedge_z A$ (see 4.17).

Let $|C|_\omega = 1$. Let ω' be a cover which, if at all, only differs from ω in z. Let C' be what is obtained from C on substitution of $\omega(x)$ for every free x; let A' be what is obtained from A on substitution of $\omega'(x)$ for every free x different from z; and let A'' be what is obtained from A on substitution of $\omega'(x)$ for *every* free x.

A'' is obtained from A' on substitution of $\omega'(z)$ for z. Now C' is of the form $\bigwedge_z A'$, and this belongs to Ω as $|C|_\omega = 1$. From axioms 5 (see 4.14) we infer that, on substitution of $\omega'(z)$ for z, something is obtained that belongs to Ω. Therefore A'' belongs to Ω, hence $|A|_{\omega'} = 1$.

Let $|C|_\omega = 0$; let C' and A' be defined as in the foregoing. Then C', and therefore also $\bigwedge_z A'$, does not belong to Ω. Hence $\neg \bigwedge_z A'$ belongs to Ω, and therefore so does $\vee_z(\neg A')$. So there is (see first paragraph of this proof) a constant subject a so that for the formula A'', which is obtained from A' on substitution of a for z, the following holds: $\neg A''$ in Ω, hence A'' not in Ω. Let ω' be the cover with $\omega'(z) = a$ and equal to ω everywhere else. Then A'' is obtained from A by substitution of $\omega'(x)$ for every free x. Hence $|A|_{\omega'} = 0$.

4.20 | As in 4.13, there follows from the last theorem the

Completeness Theorem: in the subject-predicate language every proposition that is true is also provable.

This theorem is due to K. GÖDEL (1930). The proof given here is essentially L. HENKIN's (1949).

4.21 | The theorem arrived at in 4.19 can be strengthened a little. Consider how Ω was obtained (see 4.15).

Suppose that the vocabulary is *countably* infinite. Hence there is only a countable number of formulae; so Δ_0 has also only a countable number of formulae. Thus to arrive at Γ_1 we only have to add a countable number of formulae, and the vocabulary, too, will at most be enriched by a countable number. And so on. Finally, the enriched vocabulary is still found to be countable. Hence I is also countable. So:

If the vocabulary is countable, then every consistent set of propositions is satisfiable over a countable I.

In general it holds that it is enough for I to be a set with the same cardinal number as the given vocabulary.

This is, for reasons that will be explained in the next chapter, a paradoxical conclusion.

5 | LANGUAGE AND META-LANGUAGE

5.1 | Although it is richer than the propositional language, the subject-predicate language is still insufficient. Even ordinary speech not only has predicates of subjects but also predicates of predicates. Take the sentences:

This roof is red.
Red is a colour.
Colour is an optical phenomenon.

If we accept that "this roof" is a subject, then "red" is to be regarded as the predicate. But in the next line this predicate appears as a subject of a proposition with "colour" (or "... is a colour") as the predicate (of the second stage). And then in the third line this predicate (of the second stage) is the subject of a proposition formed with a new predicate (of the third stage).

We must be cautious with those predicates of various stages. In ordinary speech, predicates of the second stage will not directly apply to subjects — "this roof is a colour" is not actually felt to be false, but meaningless.

At the present time, there is a preference to confine oneself to predicates of the first stage. To do this, "red" in the second line must be interpreted differently from "red" in the first line. The first "red" (or "... is red") will then really be a predicate, whereas the second has to be a genuine subject. But in that case a connection will have to be established between the two.

Now in logistic language we already know such a connection between predicates and subjects. Associated with the predicate F (of first degree) is the set of all x with true $F(x)$,

$$\uparrow_x F(x),$$

which we repeatedly interpreted as a subject. Hence it stands to reason also to regard sets as subjects. The second "red" is then to be interpreted as the set of all red things. Similarly, "green" is to be the set of all green things. "Colour" in the third line is therefore the set of colours, i.e., a set of sets.

If we want to consider sets as subjects, then we need not only a predicate that should be interpreted as "...is a set", but also a relation between subjects that should be interpreted as

    ... is an element of ...,

or

    $\ldots \in \ldots$

But this is still not enough. Just as it is necessary to lay down the properties of points, lines, etc. as the basis of geometry, we here need axioms relating to sets. These can be formulated in various ways. But we must ensure that the usual processes of set theory whereby new sets are created, are reflected in the present theory — e.g., that there is an empty set, that the union of a set of sets is again a set, that for every set there exists the set of subsets, etc.

We thus get a system Γ of propositions in which the predicates "... is a set" and "... is element of ..." occur; furthermore, an equality relation, ... = ... This kind of thing is called a system of axioms for set theory. The set theory will then be the Γ-theory, i.e., the whole of the propositions that can be proved from Γ.

5.2 | But this, too, is still not enough for the purpose of mathematics. Mathematics is based on the natural numbers, which can be introduced by their usual representation. We shall attach to them the predicate

... is a natural number,

abbreviated to Z. Hence the following holds:

$Z(1), Z(2), Z(3), \ldots$

We now have to axiomatize the known connection between the individual natural numbers. This can be done by means of the relation

... is successor of ...,

or in short

$V(\ldots, \ldots)$,

i.e.,

$V(2, 1), \; V(3, 2), \; V(4, 3), \ldots$

is true.

A system of axioms for the natural numbers was given by PEANO.

1) $Z(1)$.

2) $\bigwedge_x \{Z(x) \to [\bigvee_y (Z(y) \wedge V(y, x))]\}$.

3) $\neg \bigvee_x V(1, x)$.

4) $\bigwedge_{x, x', y} \{[Z(x) \wedge Z(x') \wedge Z(y)] \to [(V(x, y) \wedge V(x', y)) \to (x = x')]\}$.

5) $\bigwedge_{x, x', y} \{[Z(x) \wedge Z(x') \wedge Z(y)] \to [(V(y, x) \wedge V(y, x')) \to (x = x')]\}$.

6) $(F(1) \wedge \bigwedge_y \{Z(y) \to \bigwedge_x[(Z(x) \wedge F(x) \wedge V(y, x)) \to F(y)]\})$
   $\to \bigwedge_z [Z(z) \to F(z)]$.

In particular, the last statement is important; it is the

Principle of complete induction: Let *F* be a property of natural numbers. Suppose that 1 possesses the property *F* and that whenever a natural number possesses the property *F*, its successor also possesses that property. Then all the natural numbers will possess the property *F*.

With the aid of this principle addition and multiplication of natural numbers can be defined.

$x + 1$ is the successor to x,

$x + (y + 1)$ is the successor to $x + y$,

$1 \cdot y = y$,

$(x + 1) \cdot y = x \cdot y + y$.

5.3 | As axioms for sets and for natural numbers we chose statements which are regarded as being true in conventional mathematics. The system Γ which they constitute is satisfied by the sets and the natural numbers in the normal sense. One might therefore assume that Γ is consistent. In the constitution of Γ we may confine ourselves to a countable number of subjects. According to 4.21, therefore, Γ would be already satisfiable over a countable *I*.

This is very strange — for the Γ-theory comprises things which we normally interpret as non-countable sets. For example, the set of the subsets of the set of the natural numbers is certainly not countable (see (1.19). This conclusion is known as the paradox of LÖWENHEIM and SKOLEM. How are we to account for this apparent contradiction?

Such a non-countable set *M* must be derivable from Γ with the aid of the resources of the subject-predicate language. But, at the same time, no one–one mapping f of *M* into the set of natural numbers must be derivable from Γ with these resources. Γ is satisfiable over a countable *I* — hence, in a valuable interpretation, *M* will be interpreted by a countable set.

What emerges from this? The one–one mapping of *M*, whose existence we can establish by speaking *about* the subject-predicate language, is not derivable from Γ by means of the subject-predicate language itself.

5.4 | This is the most suitable moment to realize that, in talking about the subject-predicate language, we often have gone far beyond the scope of that language.

The subject-predicate language, as defined here, can be manipulated by a machine. In accordance with the extremely simple rules that we have laid down, a machine can successively write down the formulae. Also, a machine can be made to apply the rules of inference systematically and thus to prove one theorem after another. Will every Γ-true proposition eventually emerge from the machine?

For every series of signs that we feed into it, the machine could check whether that series meets the requirements for a formula. But can the machine also verify the truth or falseness of a given proposition otherwise than, in constantly applying the rules of inference, waiting to see whether that proposition (or the negation thereof) will perhaps emerge?

We have shown that every Γ-true proposition of the subject-predicate language is provable from Γ (at least if Γ is consistent). But here we made use of resources not available to the machine. We accounted for the use of these resources, not in the subject-predicate language, but in English. In order to demonstrate the provability of a formula we reasoned as follows on several occasions: suppose that there exists no proof for A; then this or that contradiction will arise. We showed the provability by *indirect* means (reductio ad absurdum). But by refuting "there is no proof for A", however, we do not yet produce a proof for A. But to the machine the real production of a proof for A would be the only method to demonstrate the provability of A.

Hence it would not be inconceivable that propositions which, in talking *about* the subject-predicate language, we recognize to be true, cannot be proved (and not refuted either) by the machine manipulating *in* this language. According to a famous theorem of K. GÖDEL (1931) there are indeed such indecidable propositions in every language in which the sequence of the natural numbers can be formed. This theorem is known as the *incompleteness theorem*. Later we shall outline the reasoning that leads to this theorem.

It should be noted that the difficulties discussed here do not occur if we confine ourselves to the propositional language. The completeness theorem for the propositional language can be proved with very elementary means, or in other words: the machine itself can prove the completeness theorem for the propositional language with its own resources. In general the machine cannot accomplish the same task with regard to a subject-predicate language.

5.5 | During the proof of the completeness of a subject-predicate language, we used English as the medium of communication for talking about that language. How can we make the machine, which only has the conventionally agreed subject-predicate language at its disposal, talk about this language, so that it for example can establish the provability of something? We shall consider the answer to this question later on.

Meanwhile I want to point out a pitfall that threatens us if we discuss the phenomena of a language in that same language. There is the famous paradox of the Cretan who asserts that all Cretans are liars. We are asked to decide whether, in saying this, he is lying or telling the truth. Formulated in this way the paradox is not watertight. It is better to ask: If someone says "I am lying", is he telling a lie or speaking the truth? If he is lying, then he is lying that he is lying and therefore speaking the truth. And if he is speaking the truth, then it is true that he is lying, and so he is lying.

The cause of the difficulties in which the liar involves us and himself can be traced to the fact that we are speaking about linguistic phenomena in the same language as that in which those phenomena occur. If a person whose native language is English uses nothing but French for speaking about phenomena of the English language, he cannot be trapped in paradoxes of this kind. Such a person should not say "'dog' is a noun", but "'dog' est un substantif". Not "the assertion 'Abel killed Cain' is false" but "la proposition 'Abel killed Cain' est fausse". He can never say "I am lying", for this relates to the falseness of his direct assertions made in English; instead, the assertion "I am lying" as an assertion about assertions is made by him in French, namely, in the form "tout ce que je dis en anglais est faux", and this assertion is now not affected by the valuation made in it, since it is stated in French (and not in English). Of course, the speaker may also wish to talk about phenomena occurring in the French language. For doing this he could, for example, use German, i.e.: "tout ce que je dis en anglais est faux" — "alles, was ich auf französisch sage, ist falsch". These two assertions are formally not contradictory to each other (whether they are true is a different matter).

A preciser formulation of the paradox of the liar is provided by the following sentence:

What is written in line 23 on page 94 of this book is false.

The reader is invited to analyse this for himself.

The following definition is known as J. RICHARD's paradox:

The smallest number, that cannot be defined in the English language with less than one hundred characters.

If you count the used characters, you will find that this number has been defined by a little less than one hundred characters.

Analyse this too.

What has been explained in the foregoing is known under the slogan "language and meta-language". We talk *about* a given language *in* a meta-language.

5.6 | How can we nevertheless make the machine talk about the subject-predicate language in the subject-predicate language?

From now onwards we will deal with a (countable) subject-predicate language which contains the concepts of set and equality, and the natural numbers. The system Γ consists therefore of the axioms for these concepts. From now on we shall omit the notation Γ in "Γ-true", "proof from Γ", etc.

We devise a code for speaking about the subject-predicate language which makes use of the subject-predicate language itself. To the products of the subject-predicate language we assign code numbers. To do this we utilize certain simple properties of the natural numbers.

p is called a prime number if $p \neq 1$ and p has no divisors other than 1 and p. The prime numbers

2, 3, 5, 7, 11, 13, 17, ...

will be consecutively numbered.

$p_1, p_2, p_3, p_4, p_5, p_6, p_7, \ldots$.

We now assign code numbers as follows:
to the numerals 1, 2, 3, ..., n the code numbers $2^1, 2^2, 2^3, \ldots$
to the other constant subjects the code numbers $3^1, 3^2, 3^3, \ldots$
to the variables $x_1, x_2, x_3, \ldots$ the code numbers $5^1, 5^2, 5^3, \ldots$
to the primitive nth-degree predicates the code numbers $7^{p_n^1}, 7^{p_n^2}, 7^{p_n^3}, \ldots$
Furthermore,
if f is a primitive nth-degree predicate with code number $[f]$ and $z_1, \ldots, z_n$ are subjects with respective code numbers $[z_1], \ldots, [z_n]$, then we assign to

$f(z_1, \ldots, z_n)$ the code number $11^{[f]} \cdot 13^{p_1^{[z_1]}} p_2^{[z_2]} \ldots p_n^{[z_n]}$;

if A and B are formulae (with code numbers $[A]$ and $[B]$), then we assign to

$(A \rightarrow B)$ the code number $17^{[A]} \cdot 19^{[B]}$;

if A is a formula (code number $[A]$) and x is a variable (code number $[x]$), then we assign to

$\wedge_x A$ the code number $23^{[A]} \cdot 29^{[x]}$.

Thus, to every formula (at least) one code number has been attached. In order to ascertain whether a given number occurs as a code number and, if so, to which formula it relates, we need merely resolve the number into prime factors and systematically "translate back". A machine is perfectly capable of doing this sort of thing. If, for example, there appears a 23 among the prime factors, then the number must have the form $23^a \cdot 29^b$, if it is to be the code number of a formula, and the formula must be of the form $\wedge_x A$, where A and x have respectively codenumbers a and b. These a and b are processed in a similar way, and so on, down to the subjects and the primitive predicates. "x occurs as a free variable in A" is, on coding, a numerical relation between $[x]$ and $[A]$ which the machine is able to unravel. The property of a formula of being an axiom is essentially a numerical property of its code number, which can be verified by the machine. The fact that

$$A_1, A_2, \ldots, A_m$$

forms an inference chain is expressed, on coding, by a numerical relation between the $[A_1]$, $[A_2]$, ..., $[A_m]$, which can likewise be verified by the machine. To such a series of formulae Σ we assign the code number

$$[\Sigma] = 31^{p_1{}^{[A_1]} p_2{}^{[A_2]} \ldots p_m{}^{[A_m]}}.$$

That Σ is a proof for C (from Γ) is expressed as a numerical relation between $[\Sigma]$ and $[C]$, which we shall denote by

$$[\Sigma] \text{ Pr } [C].$$

We can start the machine and let it systematically produce inference chains. We can wait and see what emerges, but we cannot give the machine a particular formula and command to seek a proof for that formula (or the negation thereof). But with the available means, we can formulate in abstract terms that a formula is provable.

$$\bigvee_x x \text{ Pr } a$$

means that the formula with code number a is provable. The abbreviation of this is

$$\text{Epr } a.$$

The means with which we have talked here about the subject-predicate language belong to the subject-predicate language. We can therefore let the machine talk about its own language according to this code. Thus, for a given formula the machine can compute its code number, and for a code number it can compute the associated formula. The machine can ascertain whether n is the code number of a proposition, or whether n is the code number of a formula with x_1 as the only free variable, etc.

When the machine has produced a proof, it can determine the code numbers of the proof and of the proved formula (say b and a respectively) and ascertain

$$b \text{ Pr } a$$

and also

$$\text{Epr } a.$$

5.7 | With the available means it is not, however, possible to formulate in a consistent language what truth is. After A. TARSKI (1933), this can be shown as follows:

We express the fact that the formula with code number n is a true (more precisely a Γ-true) proposition by the validity of the formula $T(n)$. Hence:

$T(n)$ if, and only if, the formula with code number n is true.   (1)

We now show that the predicate T does not occur among the predicates of our subject-predicate language (cannot be produced by the machine), at any rate if the language is to be Γ-consistent.

We shall consider the formulae in which x_1 is the only free variable. By means of the validity of

$F(n)$

we indicate that n is the code number of such a formula. The predicate F can be produced by the machine. Let n be the code number of a formula in which x_1 is the only free variable. If we substitute in this formula the number a for the free variable x_1, then a formula is obtained whose code number will be denoted by

$S(a, n)$.

(This is defined only for those n for which $F(n)$ holds.) To calculate $S(a, n)$, one only has to break down the code number n, and replace at certain instants 5 (code number of x_1) by 2^a (code number of a). The machine is certainly able to do this. The machine is also able to form

$S(n, n)$.

Regard this now as a numerical function which we call R. Hence

$R(n)$ = code number of the formula, which arises, if in the formula with code number n we insert the numeral n at every occurrence of the only free variable x_1.   (2)

The function R is defined for all such code numbers n (i.e. for all n, for which $F(n)$ is valid). The machine can form R and can calculate $R(n)$ for every n, for which it exists.

Assume now, that the machine can also produce the predicate T, i.e. the formula $T(x_1)$. Then this is also the case for every numeral n with the formula

$\neg T(R(n))$.

With respect to this formula the machine can construct a predicate P (i.e. $P(x_1)$), so that for every n the formula

$(\neg T(R(n)) \leftrightarrow P(n))$ is provable   (3)

We now put

$$p = \text{code number of } P(x_1).\tag{4}$$

But then $F(p)$ is valid.
Replace now n in (2) and (3) by p. Hence

$R(p)$ = code number of the formula, which arises, if in the formula with code number p (with the only free variable x_1) the numeral p is substituted for the variable. (5)

And:

$$(\neg T(R(p))) \leftrightarrow P(p))\text{ is provable.}\tag{6}$$

If now in (5) the formula with code number p is explicitly substituted according to (4), then the result is

$$R(p) = \text{code number of } P(p).\tag{7}$$

Now (1) is used, with $R(p)$ instead of n:
$T(R(p))$ is true if and only if, the formula with code number $R(p)$ is true, and this is according to (7)

$$T(R(p))\text{ true, if and only if } P(p)\text{ is true.}\tag{8}$$

But now the result is a contradiction between (6) and (8). At least if we demand that nothing that is false is provable. Hence the assumption of a truth-predicate that can be produced by the machine has been proved false.
If we demand of T instead of (1) the stronger

$$T(n) \leftrightarrow N\text{ is provable,}\tag{1'}$$

again, if N is the proposition with code number n, then the result is also

$$T(R(p)) \leftrightarrow P(p)\text{ is provable.}\tag{8'}$$

Hence in that case the machine is even able to infer the inconsistency.

5.8 | We know that the predicate Epr can be formed by the machine. Now substitute in the text of 5.7 the T by Epr. Then a priori there is no reason for conditions like (1) and (1').
But we do know

that the machine can transform a proof B for A into one for b Pr a and *vice versa*, (1'')

if a and b are the code numbers of A and B.

Write now q instead of $R(p)$. q is then the code number of $P(p)$, which is also called Q. With Epr in stead of T the result is

$$\neg\text{Epr}\,(q) \rightarrow Q\text{ provable,} \tag{6'}$$

$$q = \text{code number of } Q. \tag{7'}$$

In the course of turning out proofs, the machine can never produce a formula

$$b \text{ Pr } q.$$

For if this should occur, then according to (1″) it can immediately transform this into a proof for Q: hence according to (6′) into a proof for $\neg\text{Epr}(q)$, which is contradictory to b Pr q.

On the other hand, the machine can verify for every chain of formulae, if it is a proof of Q, hence for every b

whether b Pr q or $\neg(b$ Pr $q)$.

We saw just now that the former will never emerge from the machine. Hence the machine will find all formulae

$$\neg(b \text{ Pr } q).$$

We should therefore expect it also to find the generalization hereof, i.e.,

$$\wedge_x \neg(x \text{ Pr } q),^*)$$

or

$$\neg\vee_x(x \text{ Pr } q).$$

But this would be

$$\neg\text{Epr } q,$$

and this would mean that according to (6′) a proof for Q must emerge from the machine.

The proof B of Q could then be transformed by the machine according to (1″) into a proof of

$$b \text{ Pr } q,$$

where b is the code number of B, and this is impossible, as has been proved above.

Assuming consistency, we have found a (by the machine producible) *predicate*

---

*) Inaccurately written; one should add the requirement $Z(x)$.

Φ of natural numbers with the property that the machine can prove

$\quad$ *Φ(a) for every a*

but not

$\quad$ $\wedge_x Φ(x).$

($Φ(x)$ is $\neg(x$ Pr $q)$.)
This is the principal content of K. GÖDEL's incompleteness theorem, already referred to in 5.4. The proposition $\wedge_x Φ(x)$ is not provable by the machine, although for every a there exists a machine-made proof of $Φ(a)$.

The fact, that this unprovable proposition in a way asserts its own unprovability, should cause us to regard it as being true.

It seems obvious, to add $\wedge_x Φ(x)$ to $Γ$ as a new axiom.

Will the system then stay consistent? One should think: yes. For $\wedge_x Φ(x) \to \otimes$ means also $\vee_x \neg Φ(x)$. If we could obtain from this (for a certain numeral a) the formula $\neg Φ(a)$, then this is contrary to: $Φ(a)$ for all a. We should not however draw this conclusion so quickly, for from 4.15 we know, that it is not necessary that there exists an "example" $A(a)$ for the provable $\vee_x A$. However $Φ$ can be changed — we shall not do that here — so that the proposition $\wedge_x Φ(x)$ can be added to $Γ$ without detriment to the consistency (not so the proposition Epr $\wedge_x Φ(x)$, however). In the enriched language, however, it is again possible to find propositions like $Φ$.

5.9 | Anyway, $\neg \wedge_x Φ(x)$ can just as well be added to the language without detriment to the consistency. (For a proof of $\otimes$ from $\neg \wedge_x Φ(x)$ would be a proof of the unprovable $\wedge_x Φ(x)$). In the language thus enriched with axioms we now really have the situation that

$\quad$ $\vee_x A$ without an "example" $A(a)$ $\hfill$ (*)

(namely with $\neg Φ(x)$ for A).
According to the completeness theorem, we could add so many new constant subjects to such a language, that (*) does not occur any more. In our case these should be of course new natural numbers. But how? All natural numbers existed already in our language. Clearly PEANO's axioms make the (wrong) impression, that they completely fix the notion "natural number". We have been led here to a concept of "number", that does satisfy the axioms, and still behaves differently from the intuitive concept.

5.10 | Then why do we not prohibit those languages in which (*) occurs — for example, by adding as a rule of inference to every subject-predicate language:

if $F(a)$ for every constant subject a, then $\wedge_x F(x)$,

or

if $\vee_x G(x)$, then there is a constant subject a with $G(a)$.

Well, such a rule of inference would be of no use to the machine, for if the number of constant subjects is infinite, the machine can never complete the task of verifying $F(a)$.

5.11 | The moral of all of this is: If we formalize "all" by "$\wedge$", we try to seize the infiniteness in a finite grasp. But we are only moderately successful.

6 | SOLUTIONS

1.10

1.a. For $x \in A$ there are precisely two mutually exclusive possibilities: either

$x \in B$, i.e., $x \in A \cap B$, or $x \notin B$, i.e., $x \in A \backslash B$.

b. $A = (A \backslash B) \cup (A \cap B) = (A \backslash B) \cup \{A \cap [(B \backslash C) \cup (B \cap C)]\} = (A \backslash B) \cup [A \cap (B \backslash C)] \cup (A \cap B \cap C) \subset (A \backslash B) \cup (B \backslash C) \cup (A \cap B \cap C),$

where 1a has been used twice and a distributivity has been used once. Analogous formulae for B and C show: left-hand member of 1b $\subset$ right-hand member of 1b. The reverse is evident.

c. Analogous to Prob. 1b.
a'. See Prob. 1a.
b'. Analogous.
c'. $A = C, \ B = D = \bigcirc$.

2.a. Follows from Prob. 1a, a'.
b. Ditto.
c. See 1.9.
d. Apply distributivity.
e. $(A \backslash C) \backslash (B \backslash C) = (A \cap C^*) \backslash (B \cap C^*) = (A \cap C^*) \cap (B \cap C^*)^* = (A \cap C^*) \cap (B^* \cup C) = A \cap C^* \cap B^* = (A \cap B^*) \cap C^* = (A \backslash B) \backslash C.$
f. Follows from Prob. 2e.

3. See Prob. 1b–c.

3.12

1. $\bigwedge_x [\bigvee_y (M(y) \wedge xKy) \wedge \bigvee_z (V(z) \wedge xKz)].$
2. $\bigwedge_x [\bigvee_y (M(y) \wedge xKy) \rightarrow \bigvee_z (V(z) \wedge xKz)].$
3. $\bigwedge_{x,y} (xKy \rightarrow xJy).$
4. $\bigwedge_{x,y,z} [(xKy \wedge yKz) \rightarrow xJz].$
5. $\bigvee_y (xGy).$
6. $\bigvee_{x,y,z} (M(x) \wedge yKx \wedge yGz \wedge V(z) \wedge xJz).$
7. $\bigvee_{u,v} (M(x) \wedge M(y) \wedge xKu \wedge yKu \wedge xKv \wedge yKv \wedge uGv).$
8. $\bigvee_{x,y,z} (V(x) \wedge U(x) \wedge M(y) \wedge A(y) \wedge xKz \wedge yKz)$
   $\rightarrow \bigvee_{u,v,w} (M(u) \wedge A(u) \wedge V(v) \wedge U(v) \wedge uKw \wedge vKw).$

9. $\neg \wedge_x[(\vee_y(xGy) \wedge M(x)) \to U(x)]$.

10. $\neg \wedge_x[(V(x) \wedge U(x)) \to \neg \vee_y(yKx \wedge M(y) \wedge A(y))]$.

11. $\wedge_y(yKx \to \vee_z(yGz))$.

12. $\vee_x \wedge_y(yKx \to \vee_z(yGz))$.

13. $\wedge_z[zKx \to \vee_u(uKy \wedge uGz)]$.

14. $\vee_z[zKy \wedge \neg \vee_u(uKx \wedge zGu)]$.

15. $\vee_{x,y} \wedge_{u,v}[(uKx \to \vee_p(pKy \wedge uGp)) \wedge (vKy \to \vee_q(qKx \wedge vGq))]$.

16. $\vee_{x,y} \neg \vee_{u,v}(uKx \wedge vKy \wedge uGv)$.

17. $yKx \to \{\wedge_z[zKy \to \vee_u(uKx \wedge zKu)]\}$.

18. True, independently of the meaning of K and U.

19–21. True.

22. $\wedge_t \vee_x Z(x, t)$.

23. $\vee_t \neg \vee_x Z(x, t)$.

24. $\vee_x \neg \vee_t Z(x, t)$.

25. $\wedge_x \vee_t Z(x, t)$.

26. $\wedge_{t,x}(Z(x, t) \to P(x, t))$.

27. $\wedge_{t,x}[Z(x, t) \to \vee_{t'}((t < t') \wedge P(x, t'))]$.

28. $\wedge_{t,x}[P(x,t) \to \vee_{t'}((t' < t) \wedge Z(x, t'))]$.

29. $\wedge_{t,x}\{[P(x, t) \wedge \neg \vee_{t'}((t' < t) \wedge Z(x, t'))] \to$
$\vee_{t''}[(t < t'') \wedge Z(x, t'') \wedge \neg P(x, t'')]\}$.

30. $\neg \vee_x \neg \vee_t P(x, t)$.

31. $\wedge_x[\wedge_t Z(x, t) \to \neg \vee_{t'} P(x, t')]$.

32. $\wedge_t \vee_x(\neg Z(x, t) \wedge \neg P(x, t))$.

33. $\wedge_x[(\neg \wedge_{t'} Z(x, t')) \to \vee_t P(x, t)]$.

34. $\wedge_{x,t}\{P(x, t) \vee \vee_{t'}[(t' < t) \wedge P(x, t')]\}$.

35. $\wedge_t(\wedge_x Z(x, t) \vee \neg \vee_x Z(x, t))$.

36. $\vee_{t,x}[P(x, t) \wedge \vee_{t'}((t' < t) \wedge Z(x, t'))] \to$
$\vee_{x,t}[Z(x, t) \wedge \vee_{t'}((t < t') \wedge P(x, t'))]$.

37. $\wedge_t \vee_{x,t',t''}[Z(x, t) \wedge (t' < t) \wedge Z(x, t'') \wedge (t < t'')]$.

38. $\wedge_{x,y,t}\{[Z(x, t) \wedge Z(y, t)] \to \wedge_{t'}[(t < t') \to (Z(x, t') \to Z(y, t'))]\}$.

39. $\wedge_{x,t}\{(Z(x, t) \wedge P(x, t)) \to \wedge_{t'}[(t < t') \to \neg(Z(x, t') \wedge P(x, t'))]\}$.

40. true	42. false	44. false
41. true	43. true	45. true

46. false	51. true	56. true
47. true	52. true	57. false
48. true	53. true	58. true
49. false	54. true	59. true
50. false	55. false	60. false

3.15.

1. $\uparrow_x A(x)$.

2. $\uparrow_x [A(x) \wedge \vee_y (xGy)]$.

3. $\uparrow_x (xKy)$.

4. $\uparrow_{\lceil x,y \rceil} (xGy)$.

5. $\uparrow_t \vee_x [Z(x, t) \wedge \neg P(x, t)]$.

6. $\uparrow_x \vee_t \{P(x, t) \wedge \neg \vee_{t'} [(t' < t) \wedge Z(x, t')]\}$.

7. The second and third expression are meaningless; we can only place $\uparrow_x$ in front of a proposition (dependent upon x), not in front of something that denotes a set.

8. true.

9. true.

10. true.

11. true.

12. true.

13. false.

14. the set of all subsets of A.

15. true.

16. false.

17. false.

18. the set of divisors of y.

19. the set of multiples of x.

20. the set of common divisors of y and z.

21. the set of common multiples of y and z.

22. (a).

23. the set of prime divisors of a.

24. the equivalence class of y.

25. true.

3.17

1. ○
2. the set of subsets of A.
3. ○
4. the set of natural numbers.
5. the set of powers of prime numbers.
6. ○

3.24

1. $\curlyvee_x x^2$.
2. $\curlyvee_x \sqrt{x}$.
3. $\curlyvee_A \uparrow_x (x \subset A)$.
4. $\curlyvee_x \uparrow_y (V(y) \wedge xKy)$.
5. $\curlyvee_t \uparrow_x Z(x, t)$.
6. $\curlyvee_{x,y} xGy$.
7. $\curlyvee_{x,y} [M(x) \wedge M(y) \wedge \vee_{u,v}(xKu \wedge vKu \wedge yKv)]$.
8. $(1, 2)$
9. The predicate "… is positive"; the set of positive numbers.
10. A function which assigns to certain functions their value at 1.
11. The set of functions which retain the addition.
12. $\curlyvee_t (|\vee_x Z(x, t)|)$.

3.26.

1. $?_b \vee_a \wedge_x (-x^2 + ax + a + b < 0)$.
2. $?_t \vee_p F(x, x, t, p)$.
3. $?_p \wedge_{t,y} \{ (\vee_x F(x, y, t, p)) \rightarrow \neg \vee_{z,t'} [(t < t') \wedge F(y, z, t', p)] \}$.
4. $?_h \wedge_{t',x,p} \vee_y [F(x, y, t', p) \wedge \vee_z F(z, x, t + h, p)]$.
5. $?_x \wedge_y \vee_t \wedge_p [(Z(p, t') \wedge (t' < t)) \rightarrow F(x, y, t, p)]$.